THE TUNNEL

THE
TUNNEL

By

ERIC WILLIAMS

COLLINS
ST JAMES'S PLACE, LONDON
1951

PRINTED IN GREAT BRITAIN
COLLINS CLEAR-TYPE PRESS : LONDON AND GLASGOW
1951

TO MY WIFE

PREFACE

IN A previous book I told how Peter Howard and John Clinton escaped from *Stalag-Luft III* by means of a wooden vaulting horse. *Stalag-Luft III* was in fact the third prison camp in which these men had been held by the Germans; and in *The Tunnel* I shall tell of the two earlier camps and of other escape attempts which were not so lucky, but which paved the way for the success of the wooden horse scheme.

A prisoner's first few days of solitary confinement immediately after capture were usually spent lying on his bed making plans to escape. By the time he reached his first camp he was thinking and talking of nothing but escape. He bored the older prisoners with his constant speculation. He sought those who had already been outside, listened to their stories and discussed their methods. He learned that some of the escapers had cut their way through the wire, some had bluffed the guards and walked out of the camp as Germans, others had managed to get away during the journeys from one camp to another; but for the majority a tunnel was the only satisfactory way. So the new prisoner began to make plans for his own tunnel only to find, every time, that it had been done before ; that repeated attempts had already exhausted the few possible starting places.

In the end the newcomer drifted into a state of lethargy. He still wanted to escape, but where was the opportunity in a compound containing a thousand men, most of whom, at one time or another, had tried to get away? He turned to study, literature, art; and waited for the inspiration that, for the majority, never came.

There were some who could not wait. Because they were naturally restless, or too fond of their freedom, they could not settle down. The thought that the war was going on without them was more than they could bear. These men either made their escape, were shot by the guards or spent their years of imprisonment in a bitter struggle against the surrounding wire.

In writing *The Tunnel* I pay homage to all those prisoners who tried and failed and tried again, and went on trying until the end of the war. Above all I pay homage to those who, in attempting to escape, were murdered by the men who led the German people at that time.

The successful escaper knows only too well how much he owes to chance; he knows also that those who tried and failed are fully entitled to lay the blame for their failure in the lap of that same blind goddess. No matter how ingenious the plan nor how careful the preparation they could not budget for the odd stroke of ill-fortune that, in an instant, wrecked many months of careful planning: a horse and cart driven over the tunnel, the chance discovery of a small quantity of excavated earth, or the sudden demand for identity papers in a dockside café.

To try is always the important thing, and in this book I have tried to recreate something of the atmosphere of those anxious, furtive, often highly amusing days in which our whole lives were filled with two diverse aims; to get out of the place, and at the same time make imprisonment as bearable as possible. The prison became a crucible in which all the traits of a man's character were hardened; a glass-house in which his personality was forced, made to grow beyond his years. From this crucible, this glasshouse, the prisoner emerged; not changed, but hardened in the cast in which he would, inevitably, later have developed.

The prison camps described are *Dulag-Luft* near Frankfurt-on-Main, and *Cflag XXIB* near Schubin in Poland. The year is 1942-43.

Part One

★

CHAPTER I

PETER HOWARD lay quietly in the thick undergrowth of the German forest and listened to the aircraft engines droning away into the darkness overhead. Still slightly dazed by his fall, he was conscious only of the silence, the resinous smell of pine trees, and that he was somehow safe from the flame and noise that had filled the last twenty minutes.

At length, with great effort, he raised his head. Everything on the ground was silent, but he realised that before long the woods would echo with the shouts of German soldiers searching for the airmen, whose parachutes they must have seen descending from the blazing aircraft. Searchlights had held him until the last minute, isolating the white swinging parachute, blinding him and indicating his path of descent.

Rising unsteadily to his feet he pressed the quick-release fastener of the parachute harness, which fell clear of his legs. He tore open the front of his inflated Mae West and struggled free. Looking round him in the wood for somewhere to hide the parachute he saw a thick clump of undergrowth and, gathering the billowing silk in his arms, he quickly stuffed it beneath the brambles. On top of the white silk he put his Mae West and the heavy padded harness, covering them with the loose moss that grew like a carpet on the forest floor. He worked fast, stopping only to listen for the sound of movement in the wood. Drops of sweat gathered in his hair and ran down his nose as he worked, although it was December and the night was cold. His limbs were trembling, and he panted with the urgency of his movements. The Germans would soon be here, and he must get away.

He looked up at the sky. Checking himself by Polaris, as he had done so often in the air, he started off at a steady walk through the forest, keeping the North Star on his right hand and walking as silently as his heavy flying boots would allow. Soon he came to a narrow path and, turning south, he continued down this until he reached a wide grass fire-lane which ran straight as a ruled line through the quiet woods.

He stopped at the junction, afraid to take to the open but aware that he would walk more easily on the soft grass of the ride. The silence was unnerving. It reminded him of when, as a boy, he had climbed into the local park to poach pheasant. Then it had been the silence that had frightened him—the silence that had been so essential to his purpose and yet had been so much his enemy. Silence that could so easily be broken by a careless foot and which, when so broken, would fly to pieces at the angry shout and trampling footsteps of the gamekeeper. Now, in Germany, it seemed to him that the whole forest was waiting for him to move, listening for the noise made by his feet in their clumsy flying boots.

At first, remembering only the fire and the need to hide his parachute and get away, he had acted without deliberation; but now he began to plan ahead, to wonder where he would go from here. He knew that somewhere round him in the forest the rest of his crew would be hiding their parachutes and making their plans to evade capture. He thought for a moment of trying to find them but, still impelled by the urgent desire to get away, he came out into the open and started to jogtrot down the ride. Apart from a few bruises he was unhurt and he felt certain that given a fair chance he could reach Holland. He had obtained a "fix" just before they were attacked and he knew that he had landed somewhere north of Osnabruck—say, forty or fifty miles from the Dutch border. Once in Holland he might get food and clothes and perhaps money from a friendly farmer. The fire-lane would lead him in the right direction and would get him quickly away from the spot where he had fallen.

As he jogged along he felt, inside him, a slight loosening of the tightness, the stiffness that had seized his limbs when first the cannon shells had torn through the fuselage and the red tongues of fire had filled the blacked-out cabin with their hungry glow. He began to curse, first wildly, then comprehensively, remembering the petrol saved for Christmas, and that this was to have been the last trip over Germany before his leave. It was an easy target, a "piece of cake"—and they had to go and get shot down by a night-fighter. And yet behind his cursing he could not help feeling glad that he was out of it, out of the swaying aircraft and the sick fear of the searchlights and the flak.

It had been his twenty-fifth operational trip. At first flying had been an adventure. Men died, he knew, but it was always the other chap. It could never happen to him. His crew had managed to get through several trips without being hit, and after that he began to view the flak below with a certain familiar interest, admiring its beauty as he, invulnerable, flew among its coloured bursting lights. But as his operational tour grew longer and one by one he lost his closest friends, the thing came nearer home. Then—after a night when the aircraft had been hit, and he had smelled the cordite and heard the white-hot fragments tearing through the fabric of the fuselage—he began to dream. And that was the end of his invulnerability. He felt the metal fragments tearing into his guts. He felt the sear and scorch of the flame as he watched a fellow aircraft twist and turn towards the ground. From then on it could happen to him. From then on it was fun no longer.

To-night, he felt, they'd had bad luck from the start. On the way out over the North Sea they'd had trouble with one of the engines. The oil pressure had been reading low and the engineer, nervous, had advised them to turn back. Then the oil had regained its normal pressure and they had carried on. They had been hit by flak over the French coast on the way in; not badly, but enough to frighten them and make the inferno above the target look angrier than it usually did. That was the worst part of any bombing trip, he thought, the waiting for the target to grow near. That last half-hour, with the target in full view all the time, the cones of searchlights and the wicked, beautiful display of flak winking and flashing and changing colour, with the tracer floating up slowly like sparks from a garden fire.

They had flown into it this time, right into it. And they had flown out of it again with one engine on fire, skimming the tops of the houses as they came, nearly out of control, but clear; clear and miraculously unwounded. Once away from the bump and growl of flak and the probing beams of searchlights the pilot had extinguished the burning engine, decided to make for base at a thousand feet; and they had settled down for the long cold trip home. They had been congratulating themselves on getting out safely when the night-fighter came in to attack.

Peter did not remember much of what had happened after the rear-gunner had given the warning. The pilot, handicapped by the dead engine, had done all he knew to lose the fighter. Peter could hear his heavy breathing over the intercomm as he threw the sluggish bomber about the sky. He heard the rear-gunner giving directions to the pilot, who was doing everything he could to avoid the fighter and yet maintain his height. Several times they thought they had given him the slip, only to hear the rear-gunner say, "He's coming in again, skipper, he's coming in from the port quarter! Turn to port . . . Now . . . *Dive!*" And they heard the sudden clatter of his guns as he fired a long burst at the fighter breaking away.

For the navigator, the engineer and the wireless operator, the whole fight had been in the heavy breathing of the pilot, the voice of the rear-gunner and the clatter of his guns; in the sudden lurching of the aircraft. Sitting in the blacked-out cabin they could see nothing. The rear-gunner in his turret could see the red-hot exhaust cowling of the attacking fighter, while the pilot and the front-gunner could see the long, graceful trajectory of his tracer bullets as they sped past and over their heads. But for the three men sitting in the half-light of their cabin, the fight had come mainly through their earphones. Whenever they heard the excited voice of the rear-gunner and the clatter of his guns the wireless operator raised his fist, thumb extended upwards, and thrust out his lower lip in a gesture of supreme confidence. "Good old Mac," he seemed to be saying, "we're O.K. now—that's fixed the blighter." And Peter, huddled over his chart-table, grinned back and nodded his head.

The fighter had made several attacks and at last driven them, jinking wildly, to within a few hundred feet of the ground. A burst of machine-gun bullets, raking them from nose to tail, had set them on fire and torn great holes in the perspex cockpit cover. Inside the aircraft it had been light as day, and reeking of cordite from their own machine-guns. Everything was light and noise and the sickening smell of burnt cordite.

The pilot, realising that it was impossible to save the aircraft, had given the order to bale out

Peter remembered taking the pilot's parachute from its rack and placing it on the seat beside him, knowing as he did it the futility of his action. The pilot, acknowledging it, had raised a hand in salute and returned to his task of holding the aircraft steady while the rest of the crew baled out.

When Peter reached the escape hatch it was open, the wind tearing and howling and blowing away the smoke from the burning wing. He found his own parachute and clipped it on to the harness at his chest. With the fuselage burning fiercely behind him and the earth a few hundred feet below, he thrust his legs through the escape hatch and was dragged out by the force of the slipstream. He must have pulled the ripcord, he did not remember doing so, because the parachute opened with a stinging crack. Something hit him on the side of the head, something kicked him between the legs, and he found himself hanging uncomfortably, swinging sickeningly from side to side.

Gradually the pendulum movement had lessened, and he was able to look around him. Away in the distance he could see several more white parachutes floating slowly down. He had tried to count them, hoping that all the crew were there, but he could not concentrate. He was turning now, twisting at the end of the shroud lines, and the discomfort of the harness between his legs was becoming a pain.

Now, on foot in the forest, he tried to shut the memory of those last few minutes from his mind. To forget the flames, the noise and the fear. To lose the vision of his pilot quietly holding the aircraft in the air while the rest of the crew leaped to safety. Wally was now probably lying dead in the charred wreckage of his aircraft. The others, if they had landed safely, were somewhere round him in the forest. He regretted that he had not tried to make contact with them, but consoled himself with the thought that, alone, he would stand a better chance of hiding up.

After running and walking for several miles he came to a place where the earth road which he was now following crossed a narrow winding stream. Ahead and to his left, reflecting the moonlight, he could see a pond encircled by tall rushes and beyond this the vague outlines of a farm.

He climbed down beside the simple wooden bridge and drank from the stream, feeling the earth bank damp beneath his knees. The water, black as ink in the darkness, was soft and tasted brackish, and Peter remembered the water-purifying tablets in the escape tin in his battledress pocket. The tin box was difficult to open and he swore softly as he wrestled with the lid. He had taken a similar tin over Germany for so long that he had almost forgotten its purpose, and had collected it automatically with his navigation chart and radio instructions. He thought of Pop Dawson, the Intelligence Officer, and his vague lectures on evasion. He would have liked Pop to be with him now. He had been very good on what to do if you came down in France or Belgium, but Peter could not remember him saying very much about coming down in Germany. He himself had never thought about being shot down and getting out unhurt. Death was the ever-present possibility but the other, the half-way house of being at large or in a prison camp in Germany, he had never really considered.

At last he got the escape kit open and examined its contents: a water-bottle of thin rubber, shaped like an old-fashioned purse; a bar of chocolate, stale and already covered with whitish powder; a small brass compass; a book of matches; Horlicks tablets and some cakes of concentrated food. Incongruously among this workmanlike assortment was a packet of chewing-gum. He unwrapped the water-bottle, filled it from the stream and added two of the purifying tablets. He tied the string tightly round the neck of the bottle, fastened it to his belt and climbed back on to the earthen road.

The farm when he passed it was quiet; not even a dog barked, and Peter imagined the farmer and his family sleeping again after the bombers had gone. He walked carefully past the outbuildings, round several fields of ploughed sandy soil, and once more into the forest which stretched ahead.

He was almost enjoying himself now, his first panic resolving into a firm determination to avoid capture—to get back, somehow, to England. It was good to walk alone

B

in the forest, alone with a single clearly defined objective. A quiet, slow, lonely campaign after the noise, urgency and clamour of the last few months. He began to walk more slowly, savouring the silence of the woods.

Another wave of bombers droned their way towards England, thousands of feet above his head. He looked up, but they were too high for him to see. His young brother Roy had been flying to-night. How strange if it should be he who flew, like a homing pigeon, so far above. He imagined the crew immobile at their stations. Soon they would be crossing the Dutch coast. They would lose height over the North Sea and, as they drank the last of their coffee, would make the jokes that are always made as a bomber nears its base. Family jokes, no longer funny, but made because they expressed the solidarity of the family. His own crew had acquired that solidarity flying for hours through the darkness of the sky. Seven men enclosed in a shell of battering roaring noise, invisible to each other but joined into intimacy by the microphones of the intercomm.

He imagined the front-gunner slowly rotating his turret as he quarters the sky for enemy aircraft. Alone in the clouds, alone with his guns and the stars and the queer thoughts that enter a man's head thousands of feet above the earth. It is cold in the turret. The gunner is unable to see the bulk of the aircraft behind him. Only when he listens for it is he conscious of the sound of the engines. Suddenly there is a click in his earphones, and softly and casually, as though the man's hand were resting on his shoulder, he hears the voice of the rear-gunner talking to the navigator. Above the roar and batter of sound in the lonely turret he hears the voice as though it were his own inner self speaking, more intimate even than his own voice which, if he were to speak outside the microphone, would vanish with the whistle of the wind. The voice, disembodied, speaks softly in his ear. It says, "Where are we, Joe— astronomically speaking I mean?" and the crew laugh.

And then the pilot's voice, "Shut up, rear-gunner, we're not clear yet. Get back to your job." And the rear-gunner's reply, "O.K., skipper—just waking up the navigator." And the earphones click again, and all is silent.

The crew in the aircraft overhead would be thinking of the flarepath and boundary lights of their own aerodrome, and all the well-worn routine of the homing bomber. The final circuit before landing. The friendly W.A.A.F. driver on the dispersal truck. The sleepy ground staff waiting to bed the aircraft down for the rest of the night. Then the interrogation, and eggs and bacon in the mess.

Whatever they were thinking they were going home; while he was alone in the middle of a pine forest in Germany, slow and earthbound, ill-equipped for a journey that would last at best for several days.

The forest appeared to be endless. During the past few hours he had crossed several roads, lying for minutes listening before daring to cross; but always the forest lay ahead, silent, vast and uninhabited. "*Lebensraum,*" he muttered to himself, "I thought they needed *Lebensraum!*"

He was feeling tired now, and the heavy fleece-lined flying boots were chafing his heels. He had formed some sort of plan for the journey westward and had decided on a twenty-mile walk every night, with a good rest during the day. He must walk only at night. He remembered Pop Dawson at the end of one of his lectures: "I can't tell you much about Germany—except that you won't get help there. Walk by night and lie up somewhere during the day. Try to reach an occupied country as quickly as you can."

Until now Germany had existed for Peter only as area on the map, its towns targets and its rivers navigational aids. It had been a vast sea of blackness to be crossed as secretly as possible, a sea patrolled by night-fighters and erupting sudden bursts of flak and blinding violet light. He had known there were towns and cities there, women and children, villages and farms. But to the bomber crew Germany was primarily a chart, their target a pinpoint to be found and bombed impersonally as one would bomb a target on the bombing range at home.

He kept going until morning, walking and running alternately and making long detours across farmland to circumvent villages. At first, in the wooded country, the soil had been dry and sandy, but later he came to a more open plain, flatter and with much water. The villages were larger and more spread out, and it took longer to get round them. Once he took the risk of following the road over a level-crossing. As he ducked under the second bar he heard a voice shouting at him from a signal box which stood at the side of the track. The German words came unexpectedly out of the night, and in his panic he could not remember a word of the language. He hurried on without speaking and, once out of sight of the railway, ran for nearly a mile in his panic to get away.

When he could run and walk no longer he settled down under some bushes on the bank of a stream, to lie up until the next evening. It was not an ideal hiding-place but dawn had come suddenly. The eastern sky was already pale, and he was afraid he would not find a better place before full daylight.

At first he had been able to sleep, his head on the warm collar of his sheepskin flying jacket. Later, wakened by the cold, he had been unable to keep his legs warm. It was damp under the bushes, a dampness that seemed to strike upwards through his battledress trousers and eat into his hip-bone as he lay on his side on the sloping ground. He took off the short Irvin jacket and lay on this, cold everywhere now but protected from the damp. By his watch it was nine-thirty, the day was grey and overcast, and he wondered how he would spend the hours until darkness.

His hiding-place, concealed from the road by the thick

bushes, seemed quiet enough, but he decided that the next day would be spent well away from the road. He would light a fire and boil some water. He lay for some time thinking of hot water; in bottles, in baths, in a central heating plant. No man could live without a fire, he decided. It would have to be a thick wood, well away from the road, and a fire made of dry twigs so that there should be no smoke.

At lunchtime he ate one of the cakes of concentrated food, and sucked two of the Horlicks tablets. He refilled the water-bottle from the stream and again disinfected the water. He spent the next half-hour in removing the flying brevet and flight lieutenant's ranking tapes from his uniform, putting them in his pocket to prove his identity if he were captured.

Once during the afternoon he was nearly discovered by some boys who were playing along the banks of the stream. They were playing soldiers, but he could not make out whether the enemy were the English or the Russians. In his day it had always been the Germans. The leader of the band, a tall fair youth in abbreviated shorts—who, anachronistically, carried a sword although all his followers made the popping noise of tommy-guns or the bang of hand-grenades—had disposed his men, the Germans, among the bushes on Peter's bank of the stream, while the enemy were forced to occupy the bare sloping banks on the other side. At first there was much scouting and manœuvring for position during which Peter, pressed close to the ground in his hiding-place, prayed that they would not find him. Later, when the two armies engaged, he was able, from his vantage point under the bushes, to see most of the action. The troops were throwing clay pellets now and the British —or the Russians—were in full retreat. Half-way up the slope the fair-haired boy caught one of the enemy, a small dark child, and began to belabour him with the sword. At first Peter thought it all part of the game, but the beating was real, and the captured member finally departed for home blubbering, with blood from his nose streaming down the front of his woollen jersey. There was something frightening in the child's crying, a knowledge of persecution deeper than that of English boys, and Peter, crouching in his hiding-place, renewed his determination to stay there until it was fully dark.

He lay under the dripping bushes and imagined what he would have been doing at this moment, back at the aerodrome. It was nearly teatime. After playing squash with his brother in the afternoon he would now be lying on his bed reading a book. The batman would have stoked the cast-iron stove, and the small room at the end of the long wooden hut would be warm and quiet with the black-out curtains drawn. Only occasionally, when a Stirling on night-flying test took off or landed, would the hut shake and the room be full of noise.

He would be reading by the light of a bedside lamp and the glow from the open stove would fill the room, playing on the cream walls, on the striped Indian blanket that hung above the bed and on the few books in the dark oak shelves. From the dressing-table the photograph of Pat, strange in her stiff uniform, would look with smiling eyes at the clutter of goggles, maps, shotgun cartridges and squash balls. It had been so sudden. He felt appalled at the chaos that had been left behind for his friends and relations to clear up—the unanswered letters, unpaid bills. He knew that his room would be locked by now; that perhaps already the padré had gone through his things, thrown away those which in his opinion would cause grief to the mourning family. At first he resented this intrusion into his privacy, but saw the wisdom of it and shrugged his shoulders.

Grief to the mourning family. He thought of his mother with three sons in the R.A.F. One already killed, himself missing, Roy still flying. What did she think of at night when she heard the bombers flying out? He too had had his share of grief, he supposed. First his brother, then Pat. But he had refused to mourn. What was mourning, in the end, but selfishness. Mourning one's personal loss— that was all—pretty childish, crying after the milk was spilled.

He had been glad of the flying and the danger after Pat had died. He remembered receiving the telegram on the airfield and the rush to catch the train. How he had sat for hours in his corner seat, sending his mind ahead of the crawling train. The vision of his wife's crushed body below the rubble of the hospital, the slow maddening hours on Crewe station, where he had telephoned and been told that she had died.

As soon as darkness fell he came out of his hiding-place and hobbled up to the road. He was so stiff that he could hardly walk, but he soon got into his stride and set out strongly, glad to be on the move again.

In making a wide detour to avoid the first village he stumbled into some barbed wire and tore his trousers from the thigh to below the knee. His first reaction was one of unreasonable anger, followed quickly by an excess of misery quite out of proportion to the damage done. He hastily tied the corners of the tear together with a piece of string that he found in his pocket, and slogged on once more, seething with a bitter hatred for the German farmer who had filled his ditches with barbed wire.

He stopped later by the bank of another stream, and bathed his feet in the cold water while he laced together the edges of his torn trousers. His feet were blistered now and he had worn a large hole in the heel of each of his socks.

Just before midnight he was surprised on the road by some soldiers and girls on bicycles, but he was able to dive into a ditch without being seen. They sounded happy and warm, laughing and talking as they passed him, and he decided to steal a bicycle as soon as he could. With this in mind he explored the barns and outhouses of the next farm he came to, but he was heard by a dog which began to bark. Fearing discovery he slipped away, and took once more to the road.

As he walked the country became more and more water-logged, and whenever he had to make a detour round a village he found himself floundering, often waist-deep, in dykes and water-meadows. By now he was plastered from head to foot with mud. His flying boots were filled with water and flapped soggily round his feet.

He tried to travel as nearly due west as he could, but the road was erratic, running straight for miles and then stopping suddenly at a farm where he would be forced to take to the fields and blunder on until he found another road. He did not take to the country more than was necessary because of the waterlogged nature of the ground. Ten minutes on the road were worth hours of crawling in and out of ditches, and he sometimes walked for miles north or south in order to keep to the road.

He hummed to keep his spirits up, and tried to remember what he could of the German language. He had not learned German at school; French and Latin had been considered sufficient. He got as far as " *Gute Nacht*" and rehearsed this in case anyone spoke to him. He was lonely now, and wished that he had met another member of his crew. Even after a day and a night he was lonely, with a nagging feeling that he should declare himself to the Germans—that it was dangerous for him to live and move in the country un-recognised. It was almost as though he needed contact with another human being to prove to himself that he had in fact come out of the aircraft alive.

He did not walk so far to-night. His feet were sore, and his right shoulder and hip were stiff from the fall he had taken on landing. He was hungry, too, with a hunger that was almost a pain. He had abandoned his plans for the fire in the depths of the wood—the flat plain on which he now walked was treeless—and he settled down for the day in the loft of a barn behind a farmhouse.

The barn was better than the bushes, it was dry. He made himself a bed in the soft clover-scented hay and soon fell asleep. Later in the morning he was awakened by hunger and the sound of a horse and cart in the yard outside the barn. He lay still, listening to the rough German voices, until the cart was driven away and there was no longer any sound of life from the yard outside. It was not until the cart had gone that he realised that he had been lying stiff with fear, and that his knees were fluttering uncontrollably.

As quietly as possible he got to his feet and crept across the half-empty loft towards the square hole in the floor through which he had entered. It was an old barn, the broken wood floor roughly patched with sheets of tin, and it was difficult to move without making a noise. He lay for a time on the dry powdery wood, looking down into the barn below. Everything was quiet. There were two stalls in the barn, one obviously used for the horse, the other as a store, with piles of fodder and a heap of roots. Carefully he climbed down the ladder and searched the barn for oats; but there was nothing but hay and the roots. They were swedes, yellow and unhealthy-looking. He chose two of the smallest and took them back with him to the loft. When he tried to eat them they were coarse and hot and fibrous, and caused a thirst that made him curse himself for not filling his water-bottle the night before. He felt tempted to forage round the farmyard for water, but he forced himself to stay where he was.

Several times during the day a man wearing khaki breeches and a short black coat came into the barn. To Peter, peering through a hole in the floor, he looked as though he might be a French prisoner of war. Each time the man came to the barn he seemed more French, but Peter resisted the impulse to reveal his presence and waited impatiently for the evening.

As the day passed he began to feel the cold, even in the hay. He searched the barn thoroughly for old clothes but could not find even a sack. He stuffed some of the hay inside his battledress blouse, and fell asleep again.

Soon after dark he started on his third night's walk. His feet were badly blistered and his calf muscles had set, so that he had difficulty in walking. His tongue was like leather and he was sick several times—a thin bile that made him feel as though he had a hangover. He drank some water from a ditch by the side of the road, and thought bitterly of the chocolate he had left uneaten in the aircraft.

As he loosened up he walked more easily, but he was light-headed and careless. More than once he passed people on the road, not being quick enough to dive into the ditch before they saw him. Must pull m'self together, he thought, mustn't get caught. He ducked his head in a stream and felt refreshed.

This night he walked straight through villages. He was too tired to go round them. I'll rest up on the border, he decided, and stalk the last mile or so. For the present he felt impelled to move forward as fast as he could, his mind already grappling with the problem of crossing into Holland —an unknown country occupied by the Germans, yet holding out some hope of help from a friendly people. He tried to remember what he had been told of this border, whether it was guarded or merely submerged into the giant stronghold of Occupied Europe, but his memory told him nothing. He slogged on, driven westward by the compulsion that had driven him ever since he had landed.

In the early morning he came across some mounds in a field. In the frightening half-light of the lonely plain he thought that they were air-raid shelters, that he had stumbled on to a shadow factory or a barracks. He paused for a time, looking at them, and discovered that they were only potato clamps. He dug some potatoes out with his hands and ate them. They were old and nearly as hard to stomach as the swedes.

In his determination to reach the Dutch border as soon as possible he did not choose a hiding-place until it was too late. Dawn caught him unprepared in a bleak and empty countryside. All around him, as far as he could see, there was nothing but an unending expanse of flat marshy ground, almost colourless in the early morning twilight. Now and again a patch of water caught the light, reflecting it back, cold and metallic-looking, against the murkiness of the ground. As colour swiftly hardened from the softness of the early dawn a chill wind came from the north-east, ruffling the water in the meadows, pressing the damp serge of his battledress trousers against his legs. He walked on in the ever-increasing light, until he came to a thin hedge which grew at the lip of a wide ditch. He followed this away from the road, and crawled beneath some brambles into the most uncomfortable hide-out he had yet chosen; damp, cold and only partially hidden from the road.

He slept fitfully for about an hour-and-a-half and then, wakened as usual by the cold, he lay shivering and muttering to himself. He tried to control the violent trembling of his limbs, but it was beyond control. It came in spasms like an ague, racking him from head to foot until his limbs ached with the violence of his shivering. He wriggled his body round inside his vest, rubbing his skin against the rough wool, hoping to create some warmth from the friction. He was not hungry now. His stomach was empty, aching high up behind the diaphragm, but the thought of food made him feel sick.

He lay there until early afternoon, never fully unconscious but numb and deadened by the cold and lack of sleep. At last he could stand it no longer. He had to move. Crawling out from under the bushes he limped towards a covert that

he could see on the other side of some fields. Once in the
wood, he felt, he would be able to last out until darkness.
It was not far and he was so covered with mud that his
uniform would not be recognised. He looked round him
cautiously, but he could see no sign of life. The keen wind
that blew across the flat expanse of grey and brown countryside drove before it a thin drizzle of fine rain. He walked
on, his head bent against the wind.

He did not see the girls and the man until he was almost
on top of them. Then he looked up and saw them, a knot of
drab figures, their heads covered in sacks, loading some sort
of root crop on to a cart. Although the path that he was
following would take him within hailing distance of them,
he was afraid to turn back. It would look suspicious. He
plodded on towards them, head lowered, conscious of their
inquiring gaze, and cursing himself for a reckless fool.

As he drew abreast of them he looked up. The man was
middle-aged and wore a black cap with earflaps; his face
was dark and hard, and he had a hostile look. The girls
had stopped working and were all facing him like a herd of
cattle.

"*Heil Hitler!*" Peter said. He waved his right arm in a
vague salute. The man did not reply, and he could feel his
suspicious gaze all the way across the fields to the woods.
He had pulled his trousers down over his flying boots, but
the leather jacket was too obvious. Once under cover of the
trees he began to run, knowing in his heart that he had
thrown the game away. He knew it as certainly as if the
man had voiced his obvious suspicion.

On the far side of the covert were more ploughed fields,
and he skirted these at a shambling trot. There were flocks
of great black crows here, sleek and bloated, walking
obscenely and beating themselves slowly into the air as he
approached. He was exhausted by the time he reached a
small thicket beyond the ploughland and he threw himself
down, too spent to worry about camouflage.

When he had regained his breath he got to his feet and pushed on towards the west. He must be nearly in Holland now. Behind him, he felt, the peasant would already have given the alarm. The whole countryside would be aroused. He must get across the border. It seemed to him, numbed as he was with cold and fatigue, that once in Holland he would be safe. With any luck he could cross the border that evening and get help from a friendly farmer.

He walked on blindly, must have been walking half-asleep, because, suddenly he was in a marshy plain studded with clumps of thick bushes. In front of him was a broad river, the water cold and deep, brimming to its earthen banks. This must be the Ems, the border could only be a few more miles from here. He thought of swimming, but could not face the dank yellowness of the water and the stark emptiness of the bank beyond. Turning to his right he walked downstream until he saw a concrete road bridge springing from earth ramparts on either side of the river. He worked away from the river bank and approached the bridge from the road. It was guarded by a soldier who was inspecting the papers of everyone who crossed. This was the first enemy soldier that Peter had seen after three years of war, and he lay for some time hidden among the bushes at the side of the road, watching the stream of peasants passing the barrier.

In spite of his exhaustion he found it exciting to watch the soldier on the bridge—the well-known silhouette with its scuttle-shaped helmet and long full-skirted greatcoat. He had seen it so often in illustrations and in films that now it seemed familiar. There was only one soldier, at this end of the bridge, and after watching for some time he came to the conclusion that this must be the border. The barrier was a temporary affair and by the attitude of the peasants it seemed that the soldier was not usually there.

He made up his mind to wait until nightfall and try to cross under cover of darkness. He studied the construction of the bridge, and decided that he would be able to climb it from the river bank and edge his way across outside the parapet. He crept back to a clump of bushes below the level of the road, and composed himself to wait.

He must have fallen asleep, for it was nearly dark and he could hear German voices around him in the bushes. There were shouts and the sound of men beating the dead grass aside with sticks. He looked carefully out from his hiding-place and saw a long line of men in green uniforms, armed with shotguns and rifles. They were about twelve feet apart and were beating steadily towards him.

Once again he knew the fear that he had known as a child, a fear that he had forgotten until he started flying over Germany. The rising of the stomach, the dizziness, the nausea. Then came the sudden calmness, the desire to laugh, the joy when he had overcome the fear.

He must get out of this. He was nearly home. To get caught now would be stupid. One more effort and he would be over the border. The Germans were beating towards the river, hemming him in between themselves and the water. If he could slip quietly into the river and swim across . . . Cautiously he rose to his feet, turned round, and found himself face to face with the policeman.

He was a wizened little man in a bottle-green uniform with breeches and jackboots. Under the narrow-brimmed helmet his face was stern, his jaw set beneath a straggling grey moustache. In his hand the old-fashioned revolver, pointing uncertainly at Peter's stomach, looked incongruously lethal. He stood, a yard between them, dangerous in the very strangeness of his unaccustomed role.

Peter hesitated. There was only the old man between him and the river, but behind him were the foresters with their guns. Slowly he raised his hands above his head.

CHAPTER II

NOW THAT the hunt was over he could not help thinking how theatrical the whole thing seemed. He stood self-consciously with his hands above his head, while the policeman prodded him nervously in the stomach with the revolver. The foresters, guns levelled, stood in a solemn half-circle behind him. No one appeared to know what to do next. He half-lowered his hands, but a sharp jab with the revolver reminded him that, to his captors at least, he was an object of considerable menace.

The policeman held out his left hand. "*Papiere!*"

Peter did not understand.

"*Papiere!*" the policeman repeated, and impatiently rubbed his thumb and forefingers together.

"I have no papers," Peter said.

"*Papiere, Papiere!*" The policeman was getting angry.

Peter lowered his arms, this time with the policeman's consent, and made the motions of tearing paper and throwing away the pieces.

"*Jude!*" The policeman spat the word, his old face screwed into an expression of distaste.

Yuda, thought Peter, what the hell's *Yuda*? . . . *Jude!* Christ, he thinks I'm a Jew. "*Nicht Jude!*" he said and shook his head.

The policeman seemed to be forcing himself into some kind of rage. He scowled again. "*Roosevelt Jude.*"

"*Roosevelt nicht Jude,*" Peter said.

"*Churchill Jude.*"

Peter looked round at the foresters. He was tired and he did not feel up to a political argument. He did not feel up

to any sort of argument. Racial hatred had always frightened
him. He was frightened now that they might take him for
Jew and shoot him out of hand.

" *Churchill nicht Jude*," he said.

The policeman's attention was distracted by some small
boys who had been following up the beaters and were now
crowding in, peering with interest at the ragged and mud-
caked figure of the quarry. The policeman moved them
back and, remembering his drill, handed the revolver to
one of the foresters while he searched Peter's clothes for
firearms or a knife. He patted the pockets, under the armpits
and down the sides of the trouser legs. He found the escape
kit, looked at it and handed it back. Now that he was
certain that his captive was unarmed he relaxed, took out a
battered metal case and offered Peter a cigarette. He took
one himself and lit them both with an old-fashioned
cigarette-lighter, which he had great difficulty in working.
It was like a day's rough shooting at home. The foresters,
leaning on their guns, had retired into private daydreams
of their own. Tobacco smoke curled lazily into the winter
air. Even the small boys were quiet.

The policeman finished his cigarette, spat and wiped his
mouth with the back of his hand. It was time to move.
He motioned Peter to raise his hands above his head again
and walk towards the road.

He was marched, at the end of the revolver, out of the
bushes and down the road towards a level-crossing. It
was nearly dark, and the lighted windows of the village
looked warm and comforting. He was almost glad that
they had caught him. Now perhaps they would give
him something to eat. The thought of food made him
suddenly ill, and he was afraid that he would vomit in
the street.

By now the villagers were beginning to gather, and the
policeman formed his company into some semblance of
order. First walked two foresters dressed in green knicker-

bockers and carrying shotguns at the shoulder; then Peter, wearing mud-covered battledress, sodden flying boots and a brightly-spotted silk handkerchief round his neck. With four days' growth of beard and hands held at shoulder height, he felt like the villain in a Wild West film. During his early operational days he had always flown with a revolver in its holster at his waist. If he had this now, he thought, the picture would be complete. After him came the policeman, gently prodding his prisoner in the small of the back with the revolver. Behind them marched a solid phalanx of foresters, followed at a respectful distance by an ever-increasing crowd of curious villagers.

Half-way down the village street they were met by an Army officer. He was wearing tight-fitting olive-green uniform and badly-cut breeches whose seat was one enormous leather patch. He carried an ornamental dagger slung from his belt by silver chains and in jackboots he looked out of place on his decrepit bicycle. He dismounted when he saw the procession and stood, holding the bicycle, waiting for them to draw near.

The policeman stopped in front of the officer, bringing the procession to an abrupt halt. He raised his arm in an exaggerated Nazi salute and said, " *Heil Hitler!* "

The officer replied with a military salute. He was young, fair and pink. His blue eyes looked at Peter for a moment, but flickered away again. He spoke to the policeman in German; he seemed to be asking a question.

The policeman made a long statement. Peter lowered his arms, but raised them again when he felt the muzzle of a shotgun in the small of his back.

The officer spoke again. He ignored the prisoner, carefully not looking in his direction. Peter stood listening to the strange tongue, not understanding it, knowing that they were talking about him, and feeling acutely conscious of his beard and the jagged rent in his trouser leg. He wished that they would let him lower his arms. He was cold again

c

now, trembling, and he was worried in case the officer should think that he was frightened.

The officer and the policeman exchanged salutes, and the procession continued its triumphal march down the village street to a small hotel by the railway station.

They had allowed him to wash and now he sat in the small private room, with its stiff ancestral photographs and lace curtains, trying to appear at ease. The policeman was explaining something to him in German, but he did not even begin to understand what it was all about. At times one or other of the foresters would say something to him, apparently speaking a dialect because he could not pick out a single familiar word. The policeman had a notebook in which he had so far written nothing but the date.

When the naval officer arrived they all stood up. He was young and his face was tanned by the weather. As he held out his hand to Peter he made it an act of friendliness. "My name is Friedrichs," he said. "I have come because I speak English."

"How d'you do." Peter shook his hand.

"The policeman would like some information from you." There was the common disregard for the non-fighting services in his manner.

"I would prefer to wait until I am in a prison camp."

The officer smiled. "You are right," he said. "I would have said the same in your place." He spoke to the policeman in German.

The policeman looked disappointed. He fingered the notebook, and said something emphatically in the same language.

" He wants your name and details for his report," the officer explained. He took out a cigarette-case and handed Peter a cigarette. "I am here unofficially. I live here in the village. If there is anything I can do for you . . ."

"Where shall I be taken?" Peter asked.

The officer spoke again to the policeman. "An escort is on its way to fetch you. You will be taken to a prison camp, probably Frankfurt." He smiled. "It is not too bad. You are alive at least."

Peter did not answer.

The officer emptied his cigarette-case. "I will leave you these. You need not tell the policeman anything." He looked suddenly young and shy. "Good luck. It is all the fortune of war. You were only a few kilometres from the Dutch border."

Peter's barriers were nearly down, the dammed-up words of days of loneliness were waiting to be released to this man who spoke to him in English. But he held himself in check. They stood for a moment in silence, awkwardly, before the German, after shaking hands again, saluted and left the room.

When he had gone a girl brought sandwiches of black bread and a cup of *ersatz* coffee. She was young and dark, and when she put them on the table in front of Peter she smiled.

"*Essen*," the policeman said, and pointed to his mouth.

Peter handed the sandwiches round the table but the foresters would not eat them, urging him to go ahead. They left him alone at one end of the table while they engaged in low-voiced discussion at the other end.

He tried to eat, but could not swallow. He tried to drink the coffee but it was too hot. Once he started eating, the sandwiches vanished quickly and when he had finished he drank the coffee, feeling its bitter warmth restore his spirits. He lit one of the naval officer's cigarettes and wondered how long his escort would be.

Apparently the policeman and the foresters had reached a decision for, rising to their feet, they made signs for him to accompany them to the bar. They made him sit on a chair in the middle of the room, and opened the door to allow in a long queue of curious villagers. At first he was irritated by this, but the policeman's pride was so naïve that he could not be angry. He supposed that he was the first Englishman they had seen; so he sat there, patient but embarrassed, hoping that the naval officer would return and rescue him.

After the last civilian had left, the policeman made Peter remove his flying boots which he took and placed behind the bar. The foresters then drew chairs around the central stove and invited their prisoner to drink. *Schnapps* was poured from a large wicker-covered bottle behind the bar. They drank *schnapps* and beer, and one of the foresters smoked a pipe. Peter had a pipe in his pocket and the forester gave him some tobacco. It was light and dry and burned his tongue.

It was warm in the bar and the faint odour of stale food and beer was soon drowned in the pungent smell of German tobacco. Peter, his feet on the rail that enclosed the nearly red-hot stove, felt warm and almost happy. There was a glass of *schnapps* in his hand—six of its predecessors were already making the blood course warmly through his veins. He was happier than he had been for a long time.

The policeman was feeling good, too. It had obviously been a great day for him, a day that he would talk of here in this same bar for years to come. He meant to make it an evening worth remembering.

As he drank with them Peter wondered why they did not lock him up. Was it because they hadn't a spare room, or did they think he had shot his bolt? Or were they being courteous? He remembered wryly what the people of his village had threatened to do to any German airman that they found. Pitchforks, carving knives and horsewhips flashed through his memory. Would they really have done it? These people gave him food and cigarettes and *schnapps*. Did the people at home do the same for a German airman?

The policeman had opened his wallet and was showing him pictures of his infantry platoon in the 1914 War. He was bigger then, and had a big, serious-looking moustache. All the men were serious-looking, as though war were a serious thing in those days. Then he remembered the ancestral pictures on the wall. No, it was not war that had been serious in those days, but photography. He giggled inwardly at the silly joke.

The policeman also had an Iron Cross in his wallet; he wore the ribbon on his tunic. He was growing maudlin, and repeated over and over again a long explanation. It had something to do with the war. Peter gathered that he considered that the war had been a mistake.

One by one the foresters said " *Heil Hitler!*" took up their shotguns and departed, until there were only the policeman and two of the foresters left with Peter in the bar. One of the foresters was already drunk. He wore a shapeless hat with a tuft of boar bristles pinned to the side, and the buttons of his short green tunic were carved from horn. The other, not so drunk, smoked a pipe with a carved soft bowl which had been burned down at one side by constant lighting. It was past midnight and they had nearly finished the crock of *schnapps*.

Through a haze of fatigue and alcohol Peter saw the face of the policeman pressing close to his. The old man's tunic was unbuttoned showing a grey collarless flannel shirt and braces underneath. In his hand was the note-book. He pointed to the swastika on his tunic, and grabbed Peter by the arm. " *Nicht hier,*" he said, pointing to the badge, " *hier!*" and he tapped a forefinger on his chest beneath the tunic. Obviously he was trying to say that it was not the official who wanted the information, but the man. He had written his own name and address at the top of the page, and indicated that he wanted Peter to sign below.

Peter took the notebook. All that he was allowed to give

were his rank, name and number. He thought of Pop Dawson as he wrote: *Flight Lieutenant Peter Howard, 1174667, R.A.F., Captured by the above, 20. 12. 42.*

He remembered Pop Dawson and was overcome with shame. Here he was sitting with the enemy, drinking *schnapps* with them. He wasn't really captured yet. He might still get away. When the escort arrived he would be taken to Frankfurt—the naval type had told him that, also that they were almost on the Dutch border. He would never be nearer England then he was now. He glanced at the policeman who was putting the Iron Cross back into his wallet, at the foresters engaged in fuddled conversation. If he managed to give these chaps the slip, would there be a guard in the street, outside the door? The lavatory was useless as an avenue of escape. He had been there several times during the evening—the window was barred. There were two other doors to the bar, one leading to the private room where he had eaten and the other to the street outside. The policeman, with the flap of his revolver holster un-buttoned, sat between him and the door. Behind him was the staircase up which the girl had gone to bed; but even if he managed to reach the top without being hit, there was still the possibility of a guard outside the house. He must find out.

He would sing. He would get the others to join in, and they would make so much noise that if there were a man outside he would look in to see what all the row was about. But it must look natural. He was not the singing type; organised singsongs usually filled him with embarrassment. And it must be a song in which the others would join. It would have to be a song of the last war . . . Simulating drunkenness, he caught the policeman by the arm and began a personal, almost tuneless version of *Pack Up Your Troubles In Your Old Kitbag.*

At first the policeman looked at him with owlish astonish-ment. Then, surprisingly, he recognised the tune. (It was not until some time later that Peter learned that the Germans had their own marching song to the same tune.) The policeman sang with him in German. The foresters joined in. Peter's tuneless voice was drowned in a roar of Teutonic fervour. It was magnificent. It was just what he wanted. He beat time with his mug on the table, shouting at the top of his voice, while the policeman, the present forgotten, sang in an older war; a war in which he too had fought as a soldier.

Surely enough the door opened and a forester armed with a rifle looked in. He shouted something in German, pointed up the stairs, and withdrew.

Then the policeman passed out. Without any warning he fell flat across the table, his hands sprawling out in front of him, his absurd helmet rolling across the floor and coming to rest against the bar. Suddenly he seemed pitiful to Peter —an old man in his cups, his scanty hair lying in the spilt beer on the table top.

The foresters would have left him there—continued with their song—but Peter lifted the old man's head from the table and leaned him back in the chair. His head fell forward with a loose heaviness, his whole body limp and sagging.

"Water!" Peter said, and made the motion of throwing water in the policeman's face.

The foresters grinned. The one with the pipe took the old man's head, the other his knees, and they carried him across the room and into the lavatory at the back. For a moment Peter sat alone in the smoke-filled room. This was his chance and he must take it now. He crossed the floor silently in his socks, retrieved his boots from behind the bar and quickly climbed the stairs to the floor above. Which was the girl's room? He knew that if he went in there her screams would attract the attention of the man outside. Would there be a bathroom? If so, it was probably immediately above the lavatory.

Quietly he opened the door on the far side of the landing. This must be the back of the house; he knew that there was a guard on the front. The room was a bedroom. Inside, he could see a gigantic wardrobe and a high bed heaped with eiderdowns. There was a figure in the bed and he hesitated in the doorway for a moment listening to the heavy breathing and wondering what to do. He thought how terrified the sleeper would be, should he or she awake— and how harmless he actually was.

The window was open, its lace curtains blowing into the room, and he decided to climb through. There was no time to waste. He went in, carefully closing the door behind him. The figure in the bed was moving restlessly. He paused by a bundle of clothes lying on a chair by the bed, hoping that their owner was a man. They were women's clothes. He thought of changing into them, but the awful possibility of being caught half-dressed in this woman's room made him dismiss the idea.

He climbed out of the window, dropped on to the roof of a lean-to shed, and down into the yard below. So far there had been no alarm. He crossed the yard, clambered over the fence and landed heavily on the ground outside.

Swiftly he made for the bridge near which he had been caught earlier in the afternoon. After a brief reconnaissance, he found that it was not guarded. The barrier had obviously been for him.

He ran as fast as he could for about a mile, keeping dangerously to the road but wanting to get as far into Holland as he could before daybreak. The countryside on both sides of the road was the same flat waterlogged marsh-land that he had crossed the night before, now intersected by wide dykes; and he knew that he could not travel fast away from the road. He knew also that the Germans would be out in full force by the following morning, and he decided to declare himself to a Dutch farmer and ask to be hidden for the next few days.

The rest and the food had done him good, but his energy was short-lived. When he could run no more he lurched on painfully, his only desire to flop into a hollow in the ground and sleep.

Now that he was in Holland he could not help feeling that he had played the policeman a dirty trick. It was stupid to think this way, he knew, but his conscience troubled him. He had been drinking with them all night and had not paid for a single round. He must have become light-headed again, because he kept seeing the policeman's face. The old man seemed to be looking at him reproachfully. They could have locked him up, but they had given him *schnapps*. He was worried that the old man might be shot for letting him get away.

Just before dawn he came to a small farm behind a wind-break of trees about a mile from the main road. He hid among the trees and watched the farm for signs of German occupation. He saw two young girls of about eight or nine years old, and a woman with a shawl over her head. There were no signs of men about the place. Once, as he lay there, a German Army lorry passed swiftly along the main road, but apart from that there was no activity.

He knew that he must take the risk. Travelling like this would get him nowhere. He must get civilian clothes and, if possible, papers. His boots were soft and shapeless, useless for walking, and he did not feel capable of another night on the road.

Before approaching the farm he examined the surrounding country in all directions. With his heart beating high inside his chest he came out from under the trees, walked to the back of the farmhouse, and knocked on the door.

The door was opened by one of the small girls. He could see the fear plainly in her face as she looked at him.

"R.A.F.," Peter said, and made signs of a parachute falling.

The child ran back into the house and he followed her quickly into a large stone-flagged kitchen. Standing in the centre of the room was the woman he had seen earlier in the day. She too seemed frightened and looked at him without speaking.

"R.A.F.," he said. "British—*Englander*."

Still the woman did not speak. It seemed to him that she did not want him there—that she was trying to will him out of the house again.

He smiled a reassurance. "Peter Howard!" He pointed to his chest, "*Englander—Flieger*. Parachute." And made signs as he had done for the girl.

There was a slight loosening of the woman's stricken immobility.

"Food," he said, and pointed to his mouth.

She crossed to a cupboard and brought out some cheese, butter, black bread and a large bowl of pickled cabbage, which she put on the table. He sat down and began to eat. He heard her talking to the girl, who presently ran down the path and across the field towards the wood where he had hidden. He wondered whether she had gone for the police. There was nothing that he could do about it now.

The woman had come back into the kitchen and was watching him eat, watching him and glancing nervously out of the window in the direction the little girl had gone. He desperately wanted to make some sort of contact, to find out what her sympathies were.

"Thank you," he said. "Good!" And he patted his stomach. He was rewarded with the ghost of a smile, that made him wonder whether he had eaten their evening meal.

He finished the food and rose to his feet. The woman backed towards the door. He noticed that she was younger than he had thought, but pale and very thin. When she smiled she was almost beautiful. He wanted to make her smile again. The only way to make contact was to ask for something.

"Shave," he said, "Razor," and went through the pantomime of shaving the five days' stubble from his face. The act must have been good, for she smiled again and ran to the inner room. She came back carrying an old-fashioned cut-throat razor, a shaving brush and a cake of soap. She put these down on the table and brought a bowl of hot water, a mirror and a towel.

He looked at his face in the mirror. His dark hair was thickly matted, and the lower part of his face was covered in black stubble. There were pouches under his eyes, and the eyes themselves were bloodshot. No wonder the child had been afraid. He grinned a reassurance into the mirror and was surprised to see how white his teeth appeared against the darkness of his face.

He had not removed his clothes since the night before he had been shot down and, stripping to the waist, he washed thoroughly and began to shave. The cut-throat razor was difficult to handle, but the half-unconscious routine of scraping the familiar jaw was comforting.

He wiped the residue of soap from his chin and tried to ask the woman for civilian clothes. When he pointed to his uniform and made what he thought were the appropriate signs she merely nodded and smiled, as though he had asked her to admire his appearance. He gave it up and decided to ask the farmer when he arrived home—if indeed it were the farmer and not the police the girl had gone to fetch.

In the meantime he sat on a stiff wooden chair by the peat fire drying the legs of his trousers. His battledress blouse was steaming on the hearth. I've ruined my boots, he thought. Most of the polish had been washed off, leaving the leather white and dry-looking. Moved by some impulse of caution he took the small brass compass belonging to the escape kit from his pocket, and slitting the sheepskin lining of the left boot with a penknife he slipped the compass between the sheepskin and the outside leather. It would be safer there.

He sat in the warmth and security of the kitchen, conscious of the busy movements of the woman in the next room, wondering whom the girl had gone to fetch. The woman had seemed friendly enough, but had she really understood? Was it possible that she thought that he was German? He made a movement as though to call to her, but the language difficulty was too great. His head fell forward on to his chest and he slumped down into the chair, too tired to worry any more.

When he awoke there was a man in the kitchen; a middle-aged man who stood in front of his chair, holding a grey felt hat in his hands and peering at him through steel-rimmed spectacles. "I am the schoolmaster," the man said, "I speak a little English."

Peter stood, and they shook hands.

"Where have you come from?" the schoolmaster asked.

"My aircraft was shot down in Germany. I have walked from there."

"Has anyone seen you?"

"The Germans caught me on the border, but I got away."

"No one saw you come here?"

"No."

"When were you shot down?"

"Last Friday night." He thought, as he said it, how long ago it seemed.

"Ah, that was the big raid." The schoolmaster looked relieved. "An aircraft crashed not many miles from here. It was burning in the air, I saw it come down like a burning torch."

"What time was that?"

"A few minutes after midnight."

It may have been ours, Peter thought. "What sort of aircraft was it ?"

The schoolmaster was vague. "A bomber," he said. "A

big aircraft. The pilot was most fortunate. He was alone in the aircraft when it landed in a great lake not far from here. He was not hurt at all. He was taken by the Germans —they arrived before I could get there."

It must have been ours, Peter thought. Good old Wally. And this chap had tried to help him, too. "Have you helped many airmen?" he asked.

The schoolmaster smiled and lifted his hand in a typical classroom gesture. "No—it is better that you should not ask me questions."

"The Germans will guess that I have crossed into Holland," Peter said.

The man moved to the fireplace and stood looking into the fire. "I will move you as soon as it is dark. For the time it is best that you should sleep. The woman will dry your clothes and this evening, when it is dark, I will come for you." He spoke to the woman in their own tongue, giving her instructions; then he turned to Peter again and held out his hand. He had an odd, professional manner—more like a doctor than a schoolmaster. He bowed from the waist, said something to the child and took her mother with him out into the yard.

When the woman came back into the kitchen she motioned Peter to follow her, and took him to a small bedroom at the top of the house, a room whose sloping ceiling reminded him of his bedroom at home. She said something in Dutch and he understood that she would return in a few minutes for his clothes. At first he felt reluctant to let them out of his sight, particularly the boots, knowing that he would be helpless without them; but he realised that he could not go on alone, that he was warm and dry, and that he could sleep now while plans were being made.

He undressed completely and as he climbed into the high bed with its soft feather mattress and bulky eiderdown, he felt ridiculously safe. It was as though he had come home again.

He was asleep before the woman came to take his clothes away.

Then it was night and the woman held a candle in her hand. "*Kommen Sie!*" She was shaking him by the shoulder. "*Kommen Sie! Schnell, schnell!*" She left the candle on the chest by the bed, and he could tell by the way she ran down the stairs that he must hurry. His clothes, dry and neatly folded, were on the chair by the bed. The woman had even mended the tear in his trousers.

As he dressed he felt that everything was going well. He was convinced that it was Wally who had escaped from the crashed aircraft, and he was glad that he was safe. For himself, he was as good as home again. The schoolmaster had seemed to know what he was about. Quietly confident. Peter grinned as he dressed. He and his brother had never been "absolutely certain," but always "quietly confident." It had been part of their private language.

When he got downstairs the schoolmaster was not there. Instead, he saw a young woman dressed in a blue-belted raincoat with a dark scarf round her head. The scarf and the hair that escaped from under it were covered with fine raindrops that glittered in the light of the candle. She seemed excited and spoke to him in English.

"My husband has been arrested. He was stealing a car. They must not know that it was for you, or they will shoot him. You must go."

"Who are you?" he asked, losing in that instant all his former confidence, feeling that he had made a mistake in coming here.

"I have come to tell you that you leave the house." She turned to the woman and spoke to her in Dutch, and then to Peter in English. "This woman is already a widow and if they find you here she will be shot—and the children will be orphans. The farm will be burned. My husband . . . If they know that he was helping you . . . Please go!"

She began to gather his things together, the boots from the fireplace, the Irvin jacket from the chair. "They may be coming soon," she said. "Keep away from the roads and when you get far from here ask at another farm—perhaps they will help you. But here it is too dangerous." She pushed the flying jacket at him and compelled him towards the door.

Outside in the darkness and the driving rain he stood for several seconds without a plan. The stars that had guided him fitfully throughout his journey were hidden behind the clouds. But he had little need of their guidance now, being no longer driven towards the west. He had crossed the border but was still lonely, still without the warmth of friendliness.

He followed the lane to the main road and walked farther into Holland. Perhaps once out of the border country he would get more help. His trousers were already wet again and rain dripped down his nose and into the collar of his Irvin jacket.

He walked all that night, more lonely and cold now that he had known the comfort that lay beyond the shuttered windows that he passed.

By daylight he was still on the road, but managed to find a hiding-place between two haystacks near a farm. He lay there as long as he could but towards midday, impelled by hunger and loneliness, he decided to seek help at the farm. Looking carefully up and down the road he set out for the buildings that he could see a quarter of a mile away. Just as he was rehearsing what he would say to the farmer, he was overtaken swiftly and silently by two policemen on bicycles. It was useless to resist. He had lost the spirit to resist. They walked the few miles to the village without speaking.

CHAPTER III

HE LAY on his back in the narrow cell, trying to make maps and faces out of the damp patches which stained its lime-washed walls. He was so disgusted at having been captured that he refused to think of it. He lay on a wooden plank, and the thin grey blanket that covered him smelled abominably of ancient vomit. They had taken his flying boots and his sheepskin jacket, and he was cold. He had not eaten since early that morning and now it was late in the afternoon. The pale watery light creeping in through the small heavily-barred window fell obliquely on the bucket with its rough wooden seat, which stood in one corner of the cell. He could smell it from where he lay.

He felt sick with remorse and self-disgust. It had been too silly. A long, straight, open road; the two policemen on bicycles. He had not even tried to run for it.

There had been no cigarettes and *schnapps* this time. The cold dislike of the young policemen had been frightening. They had been to him, indistinguishable from Germans— they may have been Germans. Anyway, their behaviour had been very different from that of the old policeman of two nights ago, and he had been glad when the door of the cell had closed behind them.

He felt no bitterness against the Dutch. The interpreter had told him that for every airman discovered in hiding the *Gestapo* would shoot ten Dutchmen, For him, as the man had pointed out, it would only mean a slim chance to avoid eventual capture; for the Dutch it would mean much more.

He sighed and stretched himself uncomfortably on his

wooden bed. There would be no escape from this place, he was certain of that. Solid concrete, with a door that was inches thick. Even the bread and *ersatz* coffee that he had been given for breakfast had been pushed through a trap in the door. He would rest until they moved him again, and try to get away during the journey. He turned his face to the wall and presently he fell asleep.

He was being shaken gently by the shoulder. He had been dreaming again, at first he thought it was his batman. Then he heard a voice calling, "*'Raus, 'raus!*" and became conscious of the scent. It was like the perfume they sprayed in cheap old-fashioned cinemas. He opened his eyes. A German soldier was bending over him, dragging him from the forgetfulness of sleep to the bleak reality of his cell. He sat up and pushed the hair back from his face. There were two soldiers, both armed with automatic pistols and carrying black imitation-leather briefcases.

Peter swung his legs over the side of the bed and looked at them. They were most unmilitary-looking soldiers. The one who had been shaking him was young and dark, with an unhappy full-lipped face. He wore a collar and tie with his *Luftwaffe* uniform, and the long dark hair under his forage cap was slightly waved. The silver chevrons on his sleeve gave him a theatrical, musical-comedy appearance, but the automatic pistol in his hand looked real enough.

"You can put that thing away," Peter told him.

"So long as we understand one another." The corporal spoke surprisingly good English. He straightened himself up and put the pistol back in its holster.

The older man, who was not an N.C.O., handed Peter his flying boots.

"You must come now," the corporal said.

Peter pulled on the still-damp flying boots and followed the two soldiers out into the corridor. "Where are we going?" he asked.

D

The corporal grinned knowingly. "You will find out in good time. For you the war is over. You do not ask questions—you do not think any more. You do as you are told, no?"

"No." Peter said it flatly.

"So? Then you will find life very difficult. You will find here the German discipline."

"I should like my Irvin jacket, please." He felt that in making the demand he was making one last bid for self-respect.

"Your jacket?"

"My sheepskin flying jacket. The policeman took it from me last night with the boots."

"I know nothing of such a jacket."

"Let me see the policeman."

"I have not come here to talk about flying jackets. I have come to take you away. Now we have wasted enough time. Come!"

"I demand my flying jacket!" He was suddenly overcome with fury, more annoyed about the possible loss of the jacket than he had been about tearing his trousers on the barbed-wire. Normally an even-tempered man, he was perturbed by these sudden irrational fits of rage. He managed to control his voice. "It is military equipment and you have no right to take it."

"I have not taken the jacket."

"Then I demand to see the policeman."

"You are a prisoner. You cannot demand any longer." The corporal was getting excited, shouting and waving his arms in emphasis.

Peter raised his voice in reply. "I am an officer and I demand to see an officer of my own rank before I leave this building." It sounded silly to him as he said it, but its effect on the corporal was surprising. He turned abruptly and led the way back into the cell.

"Wait here, please. I will bring the police officer."

Peter and the other soldier stood in the cell and listened to the footsteps of the corporal receding down the corridor. The soldier looked at Peter and smiled in conciliation. Peter scowled.

The police officer, when he came, was indignant. He was a big man with closely-cropped dark hair and a heavy-jowled coarse, unshaven face. There was a mark round his head where the cap had been, and his small pig-like eyes were shot with red. There had been no such jacket, he said. The prisoner had been captured as he was standing now. If there had been such a jacket it would naturally have been returned to the prisoner. Peter saw that it was hopeless. Choking with rage, he was marched down the corridor and out into the cold early morning air.

They walked to the railway station in silence, and found that the train would not arrive for another hour. Leaving the older man to guard the prisoner, the corporal went to the waiting-room and turned everyone out on to the platform, shouting at them as though they were half-witted recruits on the barrack square. As the passengers filed out, Peter could see anger and hatred for the invader written on their faces. Some of them smiled when they recognised his uniform, and several raised their fingers in the victory sign. The corporal must have noticed this, but he said nothing. He motioned Peter into the waiting-room and stood inside with his back against the door. "The flying jacket will probably go to the troops on the East Front."

"Then you know that I had a jacket?"

"You say so." He had adopted the tone of an unintelligent mother humouring a wayward child.

Peter did not reply.

"Listen," the corporal said. "We have to travel all day together. Why cannot we be friendly and talk to one another? I would like to practise my English."

"In case we win the war?"

"*Ach*, you will not win the war. The *Führer* cannot afford to lose the war."

"It isn't entirely up to the *Führer*," Peter said.

"You should not have fought against us in the first place," the corporal told him. "The *Führer* has said many times that we had no quarrel with England."

Peter did not reply.

"We are only doing now what England has done in the past."

"It's no use talking about it," Peter said. He remembered Pop Dawson and his security lectures. They will try to get you into conversation, he had said. The only way to avoid giving information is to refuse to talk. The corporal seemed a bit phoney, anyway, his English was too good.

The other soldier came in with three cups of soup. He was rather like the old policeman in that he seemed too tired for this war; too tired and not caring enough what it was all about. He put the soup on the table, smiled nervously, and relapsed into a sort of coma.

The corporal took three slices of black bread from his briefcase and gave one to Peter. "You have not much bread in England," he said.

"We have plenty of bread," Peter told him.

"*Ach*, for the rich."

"For everyone."

"*Ach*, that is what you say." He smiled his disbelief, and bit hungrily at the bread.

When the train steamed in the corporal turned all the passengers out of the nearest compartment and shut the door leading on to the corridor. He made the other soldier sit next to the window while he sat in the corner next to the corridor. Peter sat between them. The corporal unbuttoned the flap of his holster and loosened the automatic pistol. "If you attempt to escape I shall shoot," he said.

It took them all day to get to Cologne; a day in which the wooden seats became harder, and the air of the compart-

ment more foul. At one stage Peter made signs for the older
man to open the window and let in some fresh air but the
corporal, obviously fearing an escape attempt, forbade him
to do so. On most stations there was a Red Cross buffet
dispensing free soup, and while the older soldier went
foraging the corporal, growing more and more short-
tempered, guarded the prisoner and prevented other passengers from entering the compartment. There was no
heating in the carriage, and Peter sat and brooded over the
loss of his flying jacket.

He had got the jacket without having it marked on his
clothing card, and had he survived the war it would have
been his own. It was on a hot summer night, he remembered,
and they had been bombing Duisburg. They had been hit
over the target, and on coming in to land the flaps had stuck
and they had overshot and crashed into the hedge at the
far end of the runway. The aircraft had gone up in a sheet
of flame, but all the crew had been saved; and next morning
they had indented for new flying jackets, saying that theirs
had been burned in the aircraft. The wing commander
had had them in the office, all seven of them, the pile of
forms in front of him on the desk.
   "You each lost an Irvin jacket last night?"
   "Yes, sir."
   "Are you sure of this?"
   "Yes, sir."
   "I was flying last night."
   "Yes, sir?"
   "In my shirtsleeves."
There had been a short silence, then Mac, the rear-gunner:
"We took them in case it turned cold, sir. They were all
piled up at the back of the aircraft."
   Then the wing commander: "Well, I don't believe you."
But he had signed the forms and they had each drawn
another flying jacket. Now the ones they had left behind

would be returned to stores, while those they had been wearing would go to the Russian front.

At midday the soldiers opened their briefcases, and took out bread and sausage which they shared equally with their prisoner. They drank hot *ersatz* coffee from vacuum flask water-bottles and smoked foul, loosely packed cigarettes.

Several times the corporal attempted to engage Peter in conversation, but his non-committal and conclusive replies dropped each topic still-born into the moist and smoke-filled atmosphere.

He sat, hunched up against the cold, on the wooden seat and wondered about the rest of his crew. Had they been captured or were they even now hiding up under hedges and waiting for darkness to fall? None of them spoke German; but Kim, the Canadian wireless operator, spoke French. Wally was in German hands, he knew that, but what about the others . . .

They had shared a car, the old Aston Martin without a silencer which had so often made the night hideous between Cambridge and the aerodrome. She had run on hundred-octane aviation spirit and, maintained by the aircraft's ground crew, had "gone like a bomb." What would happen to her now? He would write as soon as he could to his young brother Roy, telling him that he could have her. He felt sure that the rest of the crew would agree—that is, if none of them got back, of course. If one of them got back the car would belong to him. He imagined himself driving her again, the slim wheel in his hands and the crew piled in on top of him, the exhaust blaring defiance at the police as they roared into Cambridge . . .

He must get out of this. The thought of spending the rest of the war behind barbed-wire filled him with a sudden panic. If only he had made more of his chances while he was still free . . . He checked himself and tried to think constructively. The corporal had told him that they would

change trains at Cologne and then travel eastward to
Frankfurt-on-Main. He would try to give them the slip
during the change of trains. In the meantime he must try
to sleep and let them think that he had given up all hope
of escape.

But he could not sleep and sat with his eyes closed trying
to imagine what the station would be like and how he would
make his getaway. He thought of Waterloo and Victoria
stations with their many entrances and exits, and dreamed
fantastic chases through the subways with the guards
unable to shoot because of the crowds. He imagined himself out in the busy streets, dodging through the traffic
and burying himself down narrow alleys between tall
houses. It was a fine dream while it lasted but in the
end he found himself still in the stuffy carriage with the
corporal watching him and the soldier snoring in the
opposite seat.

He thought again of the squadron, of the soft murmuring
evenings in late summer when his crew were grounded,
and the clak-clank of the reaper in the cornfields was
stronger than the faint hum of aircraft in the sky; of nights
when he, not flying, sat in the control tower waiting for
the returning squadron. Waiting until *S for Sugar*, his
brother's aircraft, had been signalled in, and then going to
bed because he did not wish his brother to know that he
had waited up. There were ten years between them. They
had gone to the same school, but in different generations;
he, already moustached, leaving as his brother entered.
Then, years later, when he was a flight lieutenant Roy had
come, as a sergeant, to the same airfield. The wing commander had told him the day before he was shot down that
Roy had been recommended for a commission and would
soon join him in the mess.

He thought of the fear at take-off, and of how relieved he
had been when flying was cancelled for the day; of how the
fear of seeming afraid was greater than the fear itself.

Bob had packed it in. Perhaps his fear of death was greater than his fear of being thought afraid. Perhaps he was, in fact, braver than any of them. Peter had met him when they had first joined the R.A.F., on the first day. They were all lined up in front of a corporal, most of them dressed in old flannel trousers and tweed jackets. War was going to be an adventure for them—a release from civilian responsibility—and they had dressed up as though they were going on holiday. But Bob wasn't dressed like that. He was wearing a neat blue business suit and his collar was starched. He carried his spare kit and shaving tackle in a leather briefcase as though he had just left the office, having put everything in order, with all the loose ends nicely tied up and ready for someone else to take over; which was exactly what he had done.

The corporal was the bullying type, one of those big fair corporals with a pale acned face, protuberant blue eyes and an air of frustrated spite. It had probably taken him years to get his two stripes, and he knew that in a few months most of the casual civilians who stood before him would be sergeants or pilot officers—and it rankled.

They were all new to the Air Force and they were careful. It wasn't that they were afraid of the man, as a man, but they were all keen to get into aircrew, and they'd heard that a bad report, even from a corporal, was enough to get you pushed off the course. So they stood there in silence as the corporal walked slowly up and down the ranks, picking out one after another as the butt of his sarcastic wit. Finally he stood back and told them collectively what he thought of them. "Don't think that just because you're going to wear Air Force blue you're going to become a lot of heroes—because you're not. Nine-tenths of you won't get through the course anyway, by the look of you. You're just a lot of bloody conscripts to me and the sooner you realise it the better it's going to be for you " He stood glaring at them, his whole tightly-belted figure expressing his contempt for the effete civilians who were intruding on his service life.

Then Bob spoke. "Corporal," he said; and there was something in his voice that made Peter wince, some compulsion behind his words that made him wish the man would say no more.

"Well," the corporal said. "What is it? Out with it!" And he stood there arms akimbo waiting for what the soft-looking bastard had to say.

Bob was obviously nervous. His face was pale but his voice was even, and it was only when you watched him closely that you saw how hard he was driving himself to say what he had to say. But he said it. He explained to the corporal that they were not conscripts but volunteers, and he made the corporal apologise before they were dismissed and sent to their sleeping quarters. Peter thought at the time that Bob had been unwise, but admired the moral courage that had forced him to speak when the rest of them were silent.

As the week's initial training stretched into months he became very friendly with Bob, realising what a spirit there was inside the man to force him on in the way that he was determined to go. He was rather old for aircrew, he wasn't the aircrew type; he was too earnest, he worried too much. It was obvious that he would find it difficult when they came to fly. Even in those days he admitted that the thought of flying frightened him. He had only volunteered for aircrew because in that way he felt that he could do his best to help to win the war.

He proved to be a good navigator, careful in calculation and meticulous in plotting; but he worried too much and tended to "flap" in the air. He disdained the slapdash methods which often got the others round the course and back to base without knowing exactly how they had done it. He refused to cheat too, and swotted in his room at night while the others went down to the village pub.

On the eve of the final "Wings" exam they all wrote

cribs on cigarette packets and small pieces of paper to be
held in the palm of the hand. Some of them even took
their class notes in with them, tucked inside their tunics
so that they could read the answers to the questions in the
lavatory at the end of the corridor. It wasn't cheating in
the ordinary sense of the word. They weren't cheating one
another; there were no honours to be gained. They knew
that they could navigate and they just wanted to get on to
operational flying as soon as possible. But Bob didn't
cheat, he had learned the stuff.

They all passed the exam, some high on the list, others—
the lazy or those who found it difficult to express themselves
—lower down. Bob came out about half-way up the list,
but he got his wings, and he got them the way he wanted
them.

Bob and he had both been posted to the same Operational
Training Unit. They were flying Wellingtons and Bob was
working hard, forcing himself to become a first-class
navigator. But he didn't like flying and Peter could tell by
his jerky manner, his preoccupied air and the strained look
round his eyes that it was getting him down. There had
been no accidents at the Navigation School, but here at
O.T.U. there was a fatal accident nearly every week.

And then one night while Bob's crew were out on a
cross-country flight the wireless broke down, and they ran
into foul weather and lost themselves. He could just
imagine Bob checking and rechecking his course and refusing to land at some unknown airfield having failed to
complete the exercise. At last he got them home. Just as
they were making the circuit of the airfield, one of the
engines cut from lack of petrol. The pilot carried out his
single-engine procedure, but as he made his approach the
other engine cut and they crashed. Six of the crew got out
without much damage, but the pilot was killed.

He had taken Bob down to the local for a few beers that
evening, but it had been no good. Bob wasn't the type for

whom a few gills of beer would make black white, or wrong anything else but wrong. He was convinced that the whole thing had been his fault, and nothing that Peter could say would make him change his view. He pointed out that the petrol cocks were the pilot's responsibility but Bob simply said that it was his fault for getting lost, and took the whole blame upon himself.

A few days after that they strolled down to the "flights" after breakfast and, just as they arrived, an aircraft crashed on take-off. One of the engines had cut, and the pilot tried to turn, spun into the deck and burst into flames. Bob turned round, walked straight into the flight commander's office and said that he wouldn't fly again. The flight commander suggested that he went on leave, but Bob said that wasn't necessary, he wouldn't change his mind.

Afterwards he told Peter that he had always been frightened of flying but had thought he could force himself to carry on. Now he found that he couldn't, and he thought the best thing was to say so, and quit. Peter remembered telling him that they were all scared but lacked the courage to admit it. He suggested that Bob should apply for a posting as an instructor. Bob said he couldn't instruct others to do what he was afraid to do himself.

He was sent down south for a special Board. When he came back he told them that he was off flying. His papers were marked "L.M.F."—lack of moral fibre.

Peter wondered what he was doing now.

Later that evening they steamed into Cologne.

The platform was crowded, and the corporal made them remain in the compartment until all the passengers had left the train and the platform was clear. Then he drew his pistol and marched Peter down the deserted platform towards the booking hall. It was icy cold after the damp cold of the railway carriage, and Peter began to wonder whether it would be a better idea to wait until he reached the prison

camp before he attempted to escape. He was very conscious
of the muzzle of the automatic pistol a few inches from his
back. After all, he would have time to prepare in the camp,
make civilian clothes and collect food. If he got away now,
in uniform, in the heart of Cologne, he would not last for
long.

Again the corporal cleared all the passengers out of the
waiting-room, and Peter noticed that they resented the
bullying way in which they were ordered out. The corporal
treated them exactly as he had treated the Dutch, shouting
at them, ignoring their angry protestations.

An hour later they went out on to the platform to wait
for the Frankfurt train. As they stood on the platform a
train on the opposite track began to move out. It was a
goods train. Peter glanced quickly around. Two steps
would take him to the edge of the platform, four more
across the track—and he could jump on to the couplings of
the slowly-moving train. The corporal would not fire for
fear of hitting the public—or would he?

While he hesitated, the older guard stepped between him
and the edge of the platform, unconsciously thwarting his
attempt. The goods train stopped again a few yards outside
the station. Lucky I didn't dash for it, Peter thought,
wouldn't have got very far if I had.

The Frankfurt train was crowded but this time the
corporal got one of the girl porters to empty a compartment
for them. She was a big girl, blondely bulging under her
rough blue serge uniform. She wore jackboots with high
heels, rather like the Russian boots that Peter could remember
his mother wearing when he was a child.

After the train had left the station the girl came into the
compartment and chatted with the corporal. She looked at
Peter with obvious interest. He wondered if she would help
him to escape, but dismissed the idea as fantastic. She seemed
to be fascinated by his appearance and repeatedly urged the
corporal to take some course of action which Peter could not

understand. Finally the corporal agreed and, apologising in English, asked if the girl could have some sort of trinket to keep as a souvenir. Thinking that she might be helpful later in the journey he gave her a penny, a halfpenny and a sixpence; but shortly after this she left the compartment and did not return.

As the train covered mile after mile in an eastward direction, Peter felt that his chance of escape was growing more and more remote. His guards were less nervous now, and he decided to try to jump from the window of the lavatory at the end of the corridor. He had been there several times during the day and one or other of his escort had gone with him, insisting that the door should be left open so that they could watch him.

This time the corporal came and Peter, explaining that this was to be a more protracted visit, gained his permission to close the door.

As soon as he had locked the door he turned to the window. It was a rise-and-fall window and was not secured in any way. He lowered it and looked out. The train was moving quite slowly along a grass embankment. He looked towards the rear of the train. Leaning from the next window were the head and shoulders of the corporal, who smugly waved his automatic pistol in admonition. Peter grinned ruefully and joined him in the corridor. "I wanted to get a spot of fresh air," he explained.

CHAPTER IV

WHEN THEY arrived at Frankfurt the corporal dismissed the other guard and took Peter into the busy street. They waited in a queue of patient civilians at a tram stop, and he wondered at the banality of his arrival. He had expected an armed escort and at least a truck, and here he was about to travel in a tramcar with a crowd of civilians going home from work.

The corporal did not speak as they stood in the queue, and Peter also thought it better not to advertise the fact that he was English.

They stood on the platform of the tramcar, well away from the step, and swayed for miles through the soft night air that was redolent with a strange perfume, almost of incense. Later he discovered that this was the odour of burning brown coal blocks. It was to be an odour that would for ever, for him, be associated with that crowded tramcar swaying through the heart of an enemy countryside.

The prison camp, as they approached it, walking silently down the soft earth road, looked stark and hard; an arpeggio of upright posts and taut barbed-wire. There were shaded arc lamps suspended from gallows above the wire, and these cast a band of concentrated brilliance about thirty feet wide entirely round the camp. The small compound in which stood the long squat shapes of the blacked-out huts was in darkness, but searchlights stabbed and blazed across it, moving nervously in hesitant sweeps over the grey roofs of the huts, caressing the wire with their long probing fingers of light.

Sentries, muffled against the cold, stamped their feet and

scuffed the loose dust of the road outside the wire, their breath pluming like smoke in the light of the arc lamps. Outside, there was light and animation. Inside, everything was silent and in darkness.

The corporal showed his pass at the gate and they were allowed to enter—without ceremony, Peter thought, into a place with such a tenacious air.

He was left alone in a large room while the corporal went to report their arrival. It was obviously the dining-hall. He sat at one of the long tables and studied a portrait of Hitler which hung on the end wall. The *Führer* was wearing a khaki uniform that looked a size too large, but in this dim light his gaze appeared hypnotic. He became bored with looking at Hitler, and examined a notice-board which was fixed to the wall near the door. He could not read the notices, but they had a familiar look—daily routine orders.

He heard footsteps behind him and, glancing over his shoulder, saw a soldier in grey fatigue uniform, without a cap, standing in the doorway. The soldier, ignoring him, stood with eyes fixed on the portrait of his *Führer* and raised his arm in silent salute. Then he crossed to the notice-board and began to read the orders.

While Peter waited for the corporal several soldiers came to read the orders, and each of them stood with arm upraised before he entered the room. The gesture of the upraised arm, so amusing when burlesqued on the stage or screen, here had a servile, fanatical strength. It was not a formal salute, such as he himself gave the national flag when passing. It was homage to the man, febrile and frightening.

In the small grey-walled office, the corporal handed his prisoner over to a stout *Feldwebel* who sat, tunic unbuttoned, behind a wooden desk. The corporal produced a long envelope and obtained in return the *Feldwebel's* signature on a form. It was as though he had delivered a parcel. He smiled at Peter : "I go now to be with my girl in Frankfurt."

He made a curving gesture with his hands and clicked his tongue.

"All right," Peter said. "I know. For me the war is over." He began to tell the *Feldwebel* about the theft of his flying jacket.

The *Feldwebel*, who spoke English with an American accent, wrote down the story of the flying jacket in laborious manuscript; but Peter felt, as he dictated, that the matter would not get beyond this—that the man was only writing because he had nothing better to do with his time. He's as much a prisoner as I am, he thought; bet he'd be with his girl in Frankfurt if he could.

The *Feldwebel* at last laid down his pen, and took his grey forage cap from one of the drawers in the desk. He led Peter down a long passage, the walls of which were composed of two rows of identical doors. The passage was grey and airless but clean, and their footsteps were loud on its wooden floor.

As they passed door after door, Peter noticed that each carried a number above a small grille, which could be concealed by a sliding panel. Some of the grilles were covered and some were not, and outside most of the doors were shoes or flying boots, put out as though for cleaning. He also noticed that from the wall by some of the doors a small red wooden arm projected like a railway signal.

Then he heard the sound of cries from one of the cells and muffled thuds as though a man were beating the other side of the thick door with his fists; but the *Feldwebel* ignored this and continued to the end of the corridor where the gaoler sat on a wooden chair reading a magazine. He was an elderly man, bespectacled, and looked more like an attendant at a public lavatory than a soldier. He rose to his feet as the *Feldwebel* approached, and unlocked one of the doors.

"Here it is," the *Feldwebel* said. "Better get stripped down now."

"What for?"

The *Feldwebel* was patient. "I got to search you. It's my duty to see that you're not hiding arms or escape material—see?" He grinned, a mouth full of bad teeth. "Wouldn't get very far if you did escape because we take your boots at night—see?"

"I have the right to be searched by an officer of my own rank," Peter said.

"I know, I know, they all say that." For the *Feldwebel* it was obviously a well-worn routine. He was not aggressive, but Peter felt that he would not get very far with his objections. "Now be sensible," the *Feldwebel* said. "All the officers have gone home for the night. See? Besides the underclothing of the English is often so dirty that the officers don't like to search them."

As Peter undressed he had to admit to himself that there was something in what the fellow said. His underclothes were plastered with mud, his feet were filthy and his finger-nails were rimmed with black. He thought of explaining that he was not always like this, that this was the result of days and nights in the country; but he thought that the *Feldwebel* would probably know about that too.

As he undressed the *Feldwebel* took the clothes one by one and dropped them in a dismal heap in the corner of the cell, to be taken away—he told Peter—for X-ray examination. The gaoler who collected the clothes left in their place a pile of khaki uniform that smelled strongly of disinfectant.

When Peter was quite naked the *Feldwebel* made him stand astride with arms raised while he, somewhat disdainfully, carried out an embarrassingly intimate search. Finding nothing concealed in the usual places, he expressed his satisfaction and told Peter to get to bed as the light would be switched out very soon.

The noise made by the guard removing the black-out shutters from outside his window jerked him into wakeful-

E

ness. It was morning, and the sunlight, filtering in through
the obscured glass of the window, made a silhouette of
iron bars and the guard's head and shoulders as he fastened
back the wooden shutters.

He looked round him at the cell which he had been too
tired to examine the night before. It was about ten feet
long by five feet wide, and the walls were grey; plain pale
grey plaster dirtied above the wooden bunk by the heads
and shoulders of earlier prisoners. On the narrow bunk
was a sackful of wood shavings or straw, which had gone
lumpy and crackled when he moved. He had slept well
enough, but now he was stiff and raised himself painfully
on his elbow. There was a table in one corner of the cell
and a small four-legged stool. On the table were a metal
jug and a thick glass tumbler, chipped at the edge. Underneath the table was a metal chamberpot. The cell seemed
dry and clean enough, but frighteningly impersonal. It
had the smell of an institution; the smell of dirt kept under
by brute force and disinfectant. He felt more immured than
he had felt since he had been captured. The place seemed
too efficient.

He got off the bed, and gingerly pulled the rough khaki
uniform over his filthy limbs. It was a French or Polish
Army uniform, with full baggy breeches and a tight
high-necked tunic. The sleeves were too short, and he was
unable to button the breeches at the waist. They had taken
his flying boots so he sat on the bed with his feet under the
still-warm blankets. They had also taken his watch, and
he had no idea of the time. He was hungry, and wanted to
relieve himself, but he would not use the chamberpot.

The *Feldwebel* had told him that to call the guard he
must turn the knob on the wall near the door. This would
release the red signal arm outside in the corridor. He got
up from the bed, turned the knob, and went back to the bed
to wait. Nothing happened. Nothing happened for ten
minutes. He realised that once the signal arm was down

there was nothing he could do; the arm could only be put up again from the outside cell. Now he could only wait until the guard noticed it, or until he came to unlock the door if he had already seen it. He was suddenly angry again. He leapt from the bed and hammered on the door with his fists. All the frustration and anger of imprisonment were in the frantic beating on the door. He beat until his fists were sore and then, in the after silence, he heard footsteps outside in the corridor and someone shouting in German.

He hammered on the door again in a sudden renewal of blind rage. "Come on, you clot!" he shouted. "Open the door! Open this bloody door, you clot!"

"You think I don't speak English." The German accent came thickly through the heavy door. "But I do speak English . . . You call me a clot—now I make you wait, see!" And he heard the footsteps recede firmly down the corridor.

He sat down on the bed again, trembling. He could wait. He wouldn't use the chamberpot for any bloody German. Drawing his knees up to his chin he clasped his arms around his shins, and waited.

Some time later the door was opened by a soldier armed with an automatic pistol. He was a young man, with a white thick-skinned face which twitched nervously as he peered into the cell.

"Toilet," Peter said. "Wash!"

"*Toilette besetzt.*" The soldier said it impatiently.

"Breakfast," Peter said. "Food——" He pointed to his mouth.

The soldier showed his wristwatch and traced his forefinger round half the dial. "*Halbe stunde,*" he said.

"Toilet," Peter repeated.

"*Toilette besetzt,*" the soldier said, and locked the door.

Hours seemed to pass while he sat uncomfortably on the bed and tried to ignore his distended bladder. It had become a point of honour not to use the chamberpot. Eventually he heard the key turn in the lock and the soldier—angel of mercy now—filled the doorway. "*Toilette frei*," he said, and handed Peter his flying boots.

Peter hobbled down the corridor. The soldier followed, and watched him through the doorless doorway. Peter did not care. The next few seconds were pure bliss.

Back in his cell he examined the flying boots. The compass was still where he had hidden it, under the sheepskin lining. He decided to leave it there for want of a better hiding-place.

He sat there waiting for his breakfast. The minutes dragged by. He heard footsteps in the corridor again and the sound of metal on metal. By the time the breakfast got half-way down the corridor he could hear the cell doors open and close. He waited in a fever of impatience. Then he thought that they had passed his door. Perhaps he was to get no breakfast. At last the key turned in the lock and the breakfast was pushed in—two very thin slices of black bread and a small glass of pale thin tea. He cupped his hands round the thick glass and sipped his "tea." It was made from some sort of herb and tasted faintly of mint. He ate the sour black bread as slowly as he could, making each mouthful last as long as possible.

Later in the morning the gaoler unlocked the door and handed him a broom. Peter raised his eyebrows in interrogation. The man made signs that he was to sweep out the cell; but he shook his head in refusal. The gaoler took the broom and relocked the door. The cell remained unswept.

He lay on his back on the bed, and waited for lunch. The fact that he had no watch worried him. He felt that it must be four o'clock at least. When the lunch did come, he asked the gaoler the time. It was half past one.

The lunch was a plate of boiled white cabbage and three potatoes cooked in their jackets.

He lay on his back on the bed and waited for dinner. When

it got dark the lights were switched on from outside the cell and a guard came round outside the hut and put up the black-out shutters. With the shutters in place the room seemed smaller, and he had to fight down a moment's panic, hold back an impulse to hammer at the door and demand to be released.

Dinner was two thin slices of black bread and a cup of *ersatz* coffee.

After dinner the gaoler came in and asked him for his boots. As he watched him put them down outside the door, he laughed again at his original impression that they had been put out to be cleaned.

Shortly after this the light flickered twice. He thought that perhaps there had been a failure, or that they were changing over circuits; and he was unprepared when five minutes later the lights were extinguished for the night. He undressed in the darkness; but the next night, and for every night that he remained in the cell, he understood and obeyed the signal.

The next day, after breakfast, the gaoler again offered him the broom. Again he refused, and again the cell remained unswept.

One of the things about the cell that worried him most was the obscured glass of the window. The light came through it satisfactorily, but the thought of what lay beyond it—country, town or further prison—tantalised him. He tried peering through the uneven surface from every angle, but could see nothing. The window had been locked with a square key and he could not unfasten it.

The long weary day was punctuated by the meals, which served only to exacerbate his hunger, and his periodic visits to the toilet. He was rested now, and the close confinement was getting on his nerves. He remembered Pop Dawson, knew that this was being done with a purpose; but still he could not prevent himself from getting rattled. If only he had something to read. If only his eyes could follow the printed lines. Anything, anything at all to take his mind outside this box of grey encroaching plaster.

It was on this, the second day, that he learned that it was necessary to turn the knob on the wall at least half an hour before he needed to go to the toilet.

So the long days dragged on. Restless days now, days in which he blamed himself for not escaping when he had the chance, days in which further escape seemed impossible, and the future stretched out as an infinity of similar days; enclosed by narrow walls, fed like an animal in a cage. As far as he could tell, no one but the *Feldwebel* and the gaoler seemed to know that he was there. Each time the gaoler brought him food he demanded to see the officer in charge, but the man merely looked at him blankly and shrugged his shoulders.

He awoke suddenly. It was night, the black-out shutters were still up, but the electric light was blazing in his face. The cell was very hot, and the light brighter than it had been in the evening, burning itself out as though with too much voltage. He lay wondering what had happened. There were voices in the corridor—then silence. Then, inexorably, the lights went out again. He tried to sleep, but could not settle down. The cell was so hot that he threw the blankets off and lay there in his underclothes.

He must have slept, because when he awoke the lights were on again. The cell was hotter than before. He was sweating. He lay and listened but he heard nothing. Suddenly, inexplicably, the lights went out again.

The following morning, after the black-out shutters had been taken down, he tried to rationalise the events of the previous night. Had he been dreaming, or had the light really been on and the cell heated almost beyond endurance? Perhaps there had been some new arrivals, which would account for the light, and he had imagined the heat. Perhaps there had been new arrivals, and the heat had been an accident. Perhaps the temperature and voltage always built up during the night . . . Perhaps they were trying to break down his morale.

At last, on the fourth day, as he was waiting for his lunch to arrive, the door was opened wide by the gaoler who then sprang stiffly to attention. After a dramatic pause a young, blond, very English-looking *Luftwaffe* officer entered the cell. He wore a pilot's badge on his tunic, and the Knight's Cross of the Iron Cross with bar. Peter, who had been sitting on the bed, rose to his feet feeling awkward in his ill-fitting khaki uniform. "Good morning," he said.

"Good morning." The German's accent was that of the West-End stage. "Thought I'd just pop in and say how do."

"Won't you sit down?" Peter said.

The German sat stiffly on the edge of the bed and produced a packet of cigarettes. He smelled strongly of shaving lotion but even this was refreshing after the smell of disinfectant. "You flew very well," he said.

"What?"

"I said that you flew very well. It was I who had the good fortune to shoot you down."

Peter felt more at ease. This was pure Pop Dawson. "Congratulations," he said.

"It was good luck. You put up a magnificent fight. It was just fortune of war, old boy."

Peter thought this was rather overdoing it.

"I would like to shake you by the hand," the German said.

Peter took his hand, wondering when he was going to get the cigarette. Surely the cigarette came next?

Yes, Pop had been right, the German offered him a cigarette. He noticed that it was an English one.

He sat on the edge of the bed and smoked the first cigarette for days. He would have preferred a pipe, but as he inhaled he felt the nicotine release the sugar in his blood, relieve the nagging hunger, soothe his nerves.

"The Wellington is not an easy aircaft to shoot down." The German's soft insistent voice dragged him back to the subject.

"No?"

"Not with the Merlin engines. Yours had the Merlin engines, I suppose?"

"I don't know."

"You don't know?" Then the pilot chuckled, the superior chuckle of pilots the world over. "Of course—you are the navigator. I have just been talking to your pilot. He tells me that you were lost."

So Wally was here, too. Peter felt an almost overpowering desire to ask about the rest of the crew, but realised that this was what the German was angling for. Perhaps it was a trap and they were still at large. He remained silent.

"A bit off course, weren't you, coming back from Hanover?"

The German's soft, insistent voice was urging him to defend his skill in navigation. But he saw the trap. "I'm sorry, you know I can't talk about flying."

The German laughed, and Peter noticed his gold teeth. "Oh, I'm not an intelligence officer—I'm aircrew like yourself. I'm here on rest after my first tour of operations. I've been flying *Junkers 88s*. Have you tried your hand at flying?"

"I'm not allowed to discuss flying."

"Look here, old boy—I only came in for a chat. I'm not interrogating you. Good Lord, I haven't sunk as low as that." He rose to his feet, offended. "However, if you're going to be stand-offish, I'll go and talk to someone else."

Peter did not want him to go. Dangerous as he was, he represented the outside world. "I'm sorry. Naturally I'm pleased to have someone to talk to. But I'm afraid I'm not allowed to discuss Service matters."

"Well, of course not, old boy! It was just that both being fliers . . ." He allowed himself to sit on the bed again. "Now what can I do for you? I'm only a visitor, don't forget . . ."

"Well—in the first place I'd like to shave. I've not been allowed to wash since I've been here. And then I'd like something to read. And to have the window of my cell open. It gets pretty stuffy in here."

"I'll do what I can about it"—then he forgot the part he was playing—"but I'm afraid that as you're not willing to co-operate with us you're going to find things a little hard at first. Life would be much easier for you, y'know, if you would decide to be sensible and tell us the little things we ask. They're not important things, you understand—we just want them for the records we make of all prisoners."

"I'm sorry, I'm afraid I can't discuss these things."

"Very well." He was on his feet again, and this time Peter did not try to stop him. "If you choose to be obstinate I'm afraid I can do nothing for you." He gathered up the cigarettes and matches from the bed and replaced his cap. "If you change your mind, tell the guard, and I will come and see you again."

During the days that followed Peter was allowed no exercise and his diet never varied. Since his first visitor he had heard nothing from Intelligence, but now he did not worry any more. The first interrogator had so closely followed the specification given by Pop Dawson that he ceased to dread the next. He spent most of his time lying on the sack of wood shavings, which he had pounded down to fit his shape, and dreaming up fantastic meals.

For the moment there was nothing more that he could do, and it was a relief to lie back and do nothing, absolutely nothing. It was just like being dead, he thought, except that one day he would go back to it all again. Like being dead long enough to learn how lovely life can be—and then having the chance to live again. Yes, he would live again. And when he returned to life, how wonderful the simple fact of living freely.

It was pleasant, in a way, suddenly to be lifted out of life and relieved of all responsibility. It was like going sick when he was at school. Now, whatever happened, he couldn't do anything about it. Unpaid bills, unanswered letters—he was not responsible for anything any more. They all thought he was dead. They wouldn't know until he got out of the cells that he was a prisoner. When he got to the main camp he would write to his brother about the car and the garage bill. For the moment he could do nothing.

He lay for hours living his life again, as far back as he could remember. It had been an active life—he had never been alone for more than a few hours at a time. Now he could think, take stock of all that he had done. It did not amount to much; a few drawings that he liked, and a lot of friends.

He had been lucky in his friends. He took each in turn and piece by piece built up a mental picture, living again the good things they had done together. With Ian, duck-shooting on the Neston marshes, with the sky red over the Welsh hills and the cold salty water running in the dykes; Ian, with his face red as the sun, carrying the long-barrelled twelve-bore that should have been in a museum long ago. The creak of beating pinions as the duck flighted in from the sea, the slow, clean shots in the failing light and the way the chosen birds came tumbling vertically downwards, suddenly bereft of flight. It was not until he too, flying, became the target for guns on the ground that he had known what the widgeon, mallard and teal had known.

He lay on his bed and saw again in memory the long wedges of flighting duck driving steadily out to sea in the early morning. The sudden quickening of their wing beats as they saw the strange object on the ground below—almost as though they had changed into a lower gear. The breaking up of the flight as the guns spoke, the way the unhurt birds stalled, wheeled, and formed up again to fly, heads out-stretched, in silent urgency for the safety of the sea.

Or climbing with John McGowan in the Welsh hills; John, with his beetling brow and incredible endurance. Being frightened on the slippery rock-face at Tryfan; clinging to the cold grey rock and seeing Lake Ogwen like a pond below; later, in the evening, drinking beer in the Pen-yr-Pas Hotel.

Or hunting with Punch. Days when the countryside was brown and green and blue, and steam from the horses rose in clouds in the misty winter air. The smell of wood smoke and the thrilling blood-curdling summons of the huntsman's horn. He had been frightened then, his fingers dead from pulling on that iron mouth. He had known that Punch was a borer, a fool; would as soon have gone through the jumps as over them. But Punch had been a friend, and when he was shot after breaking his leg at a stone wall Peter had been miserable for days . . .

And then the war. The early days of mastering once again all that he had forgotten of trigonometry. The intricacies of navigation. The long weary months of sitting in a schoolroom, treated as a child again. The first thrill of navigating his own aircraft across country at night. The close companionship of a bomber squadron.

He remembered his first meeting with his crew. Seven men, all trained on different stations, unknown to one another; meeting to form a partnership to take them through thirty trips over enemy territory. He remembered the early suspicions, the wary summing-up of each other's capabilities. In spite of the fact that he was the only officer in the crew they had soon settled down and become good friends, working well together and surviving twenty-four of their thirty trips. He wondered again where the rest of them were; whether any had succeeded where he had failed.

Of Pat, his wife, now dead, he would not think. The hurt was too new, himself too vulnerable . . .

He thought instead of his friends on the squadron. Of Ginger Grant—good old Ginger who had tried so hard to hide the schoolboy behind the huge Bomber Command moustache and frightfully battered service cap. The cap had looked "operational" from the very beginning. It was said that the day Ginger received his first uniform he had tied the cap into a ball with string, and left it in water in the washbasin all night "to make it look operational, old boy." Ginger had certainly got operational all right but, even when he was a squadron leader with the D.F.C. and bar, you could still see the marks in his cap where he had tied it with string and left it in water in the washbasin.

Ginger had been an enthusiast with a zest for the small things in life. Perhaps he had known that he too was soon to be killed. He had met a girl at a dance in Cambridge— "perfectly wizard, old boy—absolute corker!" They had danced to a tune called *This Is No Laughing Matter*, and the next day he had gone into Cambridge to buy the gramophone record. He had brought it back in an envelope tied with paper ribbon, put it on the radiogram, turned the control knob to *repeat*, and played it continually for half an hour, sitting on the lid of the radiogram, twirling his enormous moustache and defying everyone to come and turn him off.

Then there had been the day when Ginger had got drunk in Cambridge. Missing the last train home, he had slept on the platform until the milk train at four a.m. which brought him to the local station. Finding no transport there, he knocked up the stationmaster and asked where he could sleep. It was raining, and Ginger felt a hangover looming up. The stationmaster allowed him to sleep in the signal box, and Ginger bedded himself down among a mass of brightly-shining switches and levers. His last impression before falling asleep must have been of all those

switches and levers round his head, looking rather like the
cockpit of his Stirling. Hardly had he fallen into the first
deep beer-induced slumber when a train was signalled by
the violent ringing of a bell above his head. Jerked out of
his sleep, and furious at the insistent clanging of the bell,
his only sleepy reaction was to stop the row at all costs.
This he endeavoured to do by pulling and pushing every
lever and switch he could see. It was hours before they got
the line free . . .

Soon after that Ginger had "bought it" over Duisburg.
Peter had watched the take-off; seen Ginger, fooling to
the last, with his gigantic red moustache sticking out of
the top of his oxygen mask, take his aircraft away for the
last time. No one had ever heard what had become of him.

Every morning the gaoler brought the broom into the
cell and every morning Peter refused to sweep, until at last
the cell got so dirty that he had to sweep it in self-defence.
Instead of being triumphant, the guard was quite pleasant
about it, and in the afternoon he popped his head round the
door in a conspiratorial way, a bakelite safety razor in his
hand. "Wash? Shave?" he said.

He took Peter to the washroom half-way down the
corridor. It was next door to the toilet, but he had never been
allowed there before. He saw a row of basins along the wall
and, opposite them, a shower bath. The guard gave him
the razor, a piece of soap and a brush. "*Schnell, schnell,*"
he said.

The blade was blunt, and shaving was a torture. He
scraped off as much of the stubble as he could, and was
washing the soap away as the gaoler returned. Peter pointed
to the shower. "May I have a bath?" he said.

The German shook his head. "*Nein, das ist kaput. Kalt,*"
he said. "Cold!"

"Good!" Peter said; a cold bath was better than nothing.
"*Kalt* good," he repeated.

The gaoler looked anxiously up and down the corridor, and nodded his head. " *Ja—schnell, schnell,*" he said.

Peter undressed as quickly as he could while the gaoler turned on the shower. The cold water was agonising, but glorious. He scrubbed his legs and feet, and managed to get off most of the dirt. The gaoler kept urging him to hurry, and did not seem happy until he was dressed again and on his way back to the cell.

After the bath he felt more energetic and began to explore the cell. He saw that if he could get some sort of lever he would be able to open the window. The electric light cable was secured to the wall by stout metal clips and after much hard pulling he was able to loosen one of these and prise up the window catch. The window opened inwards, and outside there were strong iron bars sunk deeply into the woodwork.

He leaned his elbows on the window frame, put his head between the bars, and breathed the cool damp air. There was a faint tang of pines and the elusive incense-like odour of burning brown coal blocks. Immediately in front of him was a football pitch, muddy and neglected, its goal posts standing at drunken angles; while beyond this the pines, tall and pink, glowed warmly in the sun. He stood looking at them for a long time until the woods merged into dusk and he shivered by the open window.

From now on he opened the window whenever he was alone in the cell and, more than once, he was only just able to close it before the door opened to admit one or other of his interrogators.

The young German pilot had been back several times, but his visits had been short and unproductive. A more frequent visitor was a bespectacled *Feldwebel* with a clipped moustache, who said that he had been a waiter in London before the war. He spoke at length on social matters, on art, on national characteristics; and of how Germany did not hate England, but was surprised and hurt when she declared war. All this again was pure Pop Dawson, and Peter was able to enjoy it without being trapped.

One day the *Feldwebel* brought him a small piece of sausage on a slice of bread. "It is time you were moved to the camp," he said. "You are losing your strength lying here."

"When will they move me?" Peter asked.

"My friend," the *Feldwebel* said, looking at him through his heavy glasses. "My friend—it is all a matter of red tape. Of form-filling. All the officers here are professors from a university. They have narrow, one-track minds and cannot see things as men of the world. They have been instructed that they must get those forms filled in—but once the forms are completed they will be forgotten. Absolutely forgotten. They will be put on a file, and nobody will ever see them again. My friend—for your own sake I ask you to fill in these forms. And then you will be sent to the main camp, where you will meet your comrades. There is too much form-filling in Germany. One has to fill in forms to obtain anything. And if you do not comply, my friend, I can see that you will lie here and rot!" There were tears in the large brown eyes behind the spectacles, and Peter had to think hard of Pop Dawson to avoid giving in and completing the form, which he guessed the *Feldwebel* had in his inner pocket.

At intervals during his confinement the nocturnal heating and light-switching routine was carried out, but he never discovered whether this was a deliberate third-degree method or merely heralded the arrival of another prisoner.

He soon learned that it was advisable to save one of the three lunchtime potatoes to eat in the evening. He kept it warm by putting it on the top of the metal radiator at the end of the cell.

One day he found he had a neighbour—by his accent an American or a Canadian—and he obviously wanted to go to the toilet very badly indeed. Each time the red signal fell

—Peter could hear it in his cell—he heard the man walk furiously up and down, cursing loudly, until the gaoler arrived with his customary, "*Toilette besetzt—Kamarad*," or literally, "Toilet occupied—friend." The fifth time that this occurred Peter heard the prisoner shout in exasperation, "Say, who is this guy Conrad? He seems to live in that place!"

His neighbour also had trouble with the interrogators, and once, at the height of an argument, Peter heard a loud thump that might have been caused by a man falling. Soon after this the American was moved away.

Slowly he became accustomed to his cell. There were times when he would have done almost anything to get out of it—times when he paced restlessly up and down like a caged animal and had to fight hard to restrain himself from shouting and banging on the door. But there were also times when he lay on his bunk lost in daydreams of his own effortless spinning; daydreams of escape more thrilling than any book, daydreams from which he had to wrench himself to deal with one of the interrogators or to eat his slices of black bread. His appetite had almost gone, his blood ran slowly through his veins, and he lived more and more in the daydream world of his narrow bunk.

He had moments of exultation too, moments when the lack of food and outside stimulus turned his thoughts inward and he caught an echo of the ecstasy of the monk in his cell or the hermit in his cave. At these times he would walk up and down the narrow cell, filled with strange joy, fostering the integrity of this single individual life which burned so brightly in that grey and cheerless place. But the mood would soon pass, and he would be cold and miserable again, anxious only to be moved into the main camp where he would discover what had happened to his crew, meet his fellow prisoners and learn something of the possibilities of escape.

Every morning he piled the table and the stool on to the bed, stripped to the waist and carried out his own routine of physical training based on a combination of Yogi breathing exercises and Swedish drill. Once an interrogator came into the cell while he was in the middle of this solemn performance and, to his delight, called in the guard and had the cell thoroughly searched.

Lying on his bed one afternoon, he noticed the shadow cast by the centre bar of his window on the wall above his head. After idly watching it move along the wall as the sun moved round the sky, he thought of making a clock. When breakfast came the following morning, he made a mark on the wall under the shadow with the heel of his boot. He did the same for the midday and the evening meals. He subdivided the sections between these marks, and the clock was complete. Then he discovered that the meals did not always arrive at the same time; sometimes they were an hour early or an hour late. So he destroyed the clock.

He made a jigsaw puzzle by tearing a sheet of paper into small irregular pieces and trying to fit them together again; but this occupation was so pointless that he threw the paper away in disgust.

And at intervals the interrogators came and questioned him, or engaged him in apparently innocent conversation which always seemed at last to lead back to the forbidden topic.

On the tenth morning—he had counted them by scoring lines on the windowsill with the metal clip that he had torn from the wall—the gaoler brought him a book. It was a long book, and he began to read it carefully. He felt that he would be there for a long time, so he read every word, refusing to skip to get the sense as he usually did. He lingered over every line, seeking the author's intention, appreciating his choice of words, living intensely the lives of the characters in the book.

F

He had just finished the fourth chapter when a guard came to return his uniform and tell him to get ready to go across to the main camp, and he was surprised to find that he did not want to go. The cell had become a known, familiar place, had changed imperceptibly from a prison into a refuge. He asked if he could take the book with him, but was told that this was "*streng verboten.*"

Standing in the corridor, ready to go with him to the main camp, were some dozen other prisoners. He glanced swiftly at their faces, but saw none of his crew nor anyone he recognised. They were dressed in every sort of uniform from R.A.F. blue battledress to khaki bush-shirts and shorts, from flying boots to wooden clogs; but they were alike in their pallor and unkempt appearance.

After some shuffling about they were all assembled in a long straggling line and marched between armed guards out into the strong light of the open compound.

CHAPTER V

IT WAS exciting to be out in the open air again, after the close disinfected atmosphere of the cell. The air was hard and cool, strong with the scent of the pine forests which surrounded the camp. Surprisingly, the ground was covered with snow, and shouting children on skis swooped round them as they marched the few hundred yards down to the camp in the valley below. There was a lot of talking among the prisoners. Peter heard snatches of excuse and explanation. "So we just nipped across to look at Hamburg on the way back——" "——pumped us full of lead——" "——navigator took us smack over Cologne." "There we were, light as bloody day——" "——tried to fight our way out of it but——" "Absolutely useless——"

For himself, he did not want to talk. The spell of solitary confinement had dried his flow of speech instead of damming it. For the moment he did not care if he never spoke of flying again.

By his side a young Army officer, a captain in khaki battledress, wearing a fringe of soft dark beard, hummed quietly to himself, also withdrawn from the crossfire of verbal cannon shells.

Lining the road were wooden houses built like Swiss chalets, with balconies extending the whole length of the house. They were toylike with their high-pitched roofs and carved wooden gables, and Peter would have liked to stop and look inside. He imagined what the interior would be—the chequered linen and the honest wooden furniture.

The new arrivals were met at the gates of the compound by a small reception committee of older prisoners. There were three of them, three uncouth figures standing in the black slush of the compound waiting to welcome the new unfortunates. The first—he seemed to be in charge—was a portly middle-aged man wearing a round knitted hat, a khaki cloak fastened at the neck with a metal clip and wooden clogs. He introduced himself as the British adjutant; the other two, he said, were the doctor and the padre.

While the others were shaking hands Peter looked round him at the long green wooden huts, with their snow-covered roofs, the high double-fenced barbed-wire and the raised sentry boxes above the wire. As they stood there, a British soldier, brawny in his collarless khaki shirt, came from behind one of the huts, dragging a strange-looking wooden cart piled high with empty boxes. He spoke in German to the greatcoated guard at the gate. He spoke abruptly, obviously telling him to open the gate and to look sharp about it. The guard obeyed with surprising docility.

"Come in, boys, come in," the padre was saying with practised heartiness. He was lean and wore an R.A.F. tunic with pilot's wings, khaki breeches and flying boots. He was a squadron leader. "You're just in time for a cup of tea."

He led them into the nearest hut, which seemed to be the camp theatre. It had a raised stage at one end, but was now set out as a dining-room with forms and long trestle tables. They went through this to a smaller room, also a dining-room but with smaller tables and white tablecloths.

"This is the officers' mess," the adjutant told them. "The men eat in the larger room." He hastily corrected himself: "The transit officers' mess, that is. The permanent staff feed in another hut." It had a familiar ring to Peter; even here, in the heart of the enemy country, the racket system seemed rife. He half wished himself back in the cell again.

They each took a thick pottery mug from the table and drew tea from a large enamelled urn. The tea was strong and sweet.

"Good Lord, real tea," someone said.

"It comes in the Red Cross parcels," the adjutant explained. "Helps to keep the cold out. The grub's not bad really. We don't get enough of it, but what there is isn't bad. We have communal messing here"—he seemed rather on the defensive about this—"the food is cooked by orderlies and served in this hut. You'll be here for about ten days, then you'll be sent on to a permanent camp. This place is only a transit camp."

"What are the chances of escape from here?" It was the young Army officer.

"Not a hope, old boy. Even if you got out of the camp, this snow would give you away. You'd leave tracks wherever you went. No—I shouldn't think about it from here. Wait till you get to the permanent camp. Wait till summer— you'd not get far in this weather . . . What are things like in England? Where were you shot down?"

"Libya."

"What were you flying?"

There was a gleam of amusement in the dark eyes above the downy beard. "A B.S.A."

The adjutant looked nonplussed for a moment. He looked at the slim figure in khaki battledress, and slowly realised. "Oh—you're in the Army!" There was a world of condescension in the fruity voice. "How on earth did you get here?" The blue eyes stared frostily from above the small nose and bristling moustache.

The captain shrugged his shoulders.

"Oh, well, you are here now," the padre said. He turned to Peter. "When were you captured, lad?"

Peter told him the seventeeth of December.

"So you had Christmas in the cooler, eh?"

Peter thought over his time in the cell, trying to disentangle one day from another, decide which of them had been Christmas Day. They all ran together, forming a long chain of eventless monotonous days and nights. He could not get them into their proper sequence, and eventually he gave it up. "I suppose I did. But it wasn't any different from any other day."

"No days are any different here," the doctor sighed and sat straddle-legged on one of the benches. "I've been here for eighteen months. Sometimes it seems like eighteen years, sometimes only eighteen days. It's amazing how the time flies once you settle down."

"I thought this was a transit camp." It was the Army captain again; his tone was cool.

"We're the Permanent Staff. We pass you chaps on to the pukka camp. We were the first to arrive, so we got the job."

The captain looked at him over the rim of his cup, but said nothing.

"What are the pukka camps like?" Peter asked.

"Some good, some bad," the adjutant told him. "If you go to a good one you'll get games, theatre shows, decent huts to live in—they're not at all bad, really."

"Have you ever been in one?" the captain asked.

"Er—no, we get reports. Er—have another cup of tea?"

"We had a very good attendance on Christmas Day," the padre had Peter by the arm. "Are you a regular communicant?"

"I'm an O.D.," Peter said, and lost himself in the crowd.

When they had finished their tea, the adjutant took them to a locked room where military clothing was stacked on shelves from floor to ceiling. He gave them each a toothbrush, a cake of soap, a towel, some woollen underclothes, a pullover and an R.A.F. greatcoat. He parted with these things reluctantly as though they were his private property. "They're sent out by the Red Cross," he explained. "I'll get you to sign for them, as I expect they'll be entered against your account at home. Now I expect you'd like a bath."

The water was hot. Peter stripped off his dirty underclothes and stood under the shower for about twenty minutes, soaping himself and letting the hot water run over his head and down his back. The room became full of steam from the dozen showers. Pink figures ran shouting across the slatted floor. The sound of falling water mingled with snatches of song. He felt happy again. If they could get a shower like this every day things wouldn't be too bad. He made the most of it, fearing that it would be a weekly affair. He stood under the hot water until he was thoroughly soaked and pink all over from the heat, then turned on the cold water until he was gasping and spluttering. He dried himself on his new towel, and went across to the washbasin standing against the wall and cleaned his teeth with the new toothbrush. He brushed for about ten minutes; and then he shaved, shaved as carefully as he would have done if he had been going to a dance in the Mess. It was grand, this shave with a new blade, grand to feel the stiff bristles melt into nothing before the razor. After shaving he dressed in the clean underclothes and went back to the room where, the adjutant had told him, he would find a bed.

There were six beds in the room, and on one of them the Army captain was sitting, drying his hair.

"Is there a spare bed?" Peter asked.

"They're all spare, I think." He stopped rubbing his head. "I thought I'd have this one. But I don't mind, if you'd rather be near the door."

"No, it's all right, thanks," Peter told him, "I'll take this." He put his clothes on one of the beds near the window. "My name's Howard, Peter Howard."

"I'm John Clinton. I say—what sort of dump is this?"

"In what way?"

"This 'permanent staff' business. I've been talking to one of the chaps who's been here a few days. He says that they feed in a mess of their own—special rations and everything. Permanent staff! They look it too, I must say.

That bloody adjutant was fairly dripping with fat." He sat, young and indignant, holding the towel between his slim brown hands. He seemed too warm, too vital to be kept for long in this sterile atmosphere.

At first Peter felt an impulse to defend his own service against this attack from the Army, but the captain's indignation was without rancour. He grinned instead. "I thought you didn't altogether approve."

"It's his damned defeatist attitude," Clinton said, "telling us not to escape from here, indeed. Frightened it'd upset his precious routine, I expect." He sat on the edge of the bed, his black hair standing on end, angrily tying the laces of his suède desert boots. "Permanent staff, indeed."

"He's right in a way, you know," Peter said. "We wouldn't get far with all this snow on the ground."

"That's just an excuse, but it becomes an attitude of mind if you're not careful." He rose to his feet and began to rearrange the blankets on his bed. "I'm getting out of this as soon as I get the chance."

"I wouldn't be too optimistic," Peter said.

As he walked along to the end hut where, the adjutant had told him, he would find his crew, Peter thought of John Clinton and his youthful indignation. He had been like that himself, once. But now, at thirty, he had grown more tolerant. He found it difficult enough to drive himself at times without the added task of driving others. Clinton could not be more than twenty-two or three, he decided. Straight from school into the Army, probably.

He found his crew crowded together into a small room with ten other sergeants. The place seemed full of two-tier metal bunks and had a fire burning fiercely in the cast-iron stove. It was unbearably hot and smelled of old socks, drying uniforms and closely-crowded humanity.

Mac, the New Zealand rear-gunner, was the first to see him. "Pete!" he said. "Hey chaps, look who's here!"

Peter went in. All his crew were there, and he was glad to be with them, but embarrassed because as an officer his living conditions were so much better than theirs. He had felt this embarrassment in England where—although they had shared the same crew-room and flown in the same aircraft—social distinctions had ordained that they should eat and sleep in different Messes. Here, surrounded by their enemies, it seemed even more absurd.

Wally made a place for him near the stove. He was cooking something in a tin, which he stirred at intervals with a piece of wood. "We were just talking about you, Pete," he said. "We thought you must have made it." He turned back to the tin again; earnest, methodical Wally, as interested in the brew he was making as he would have been in flying his aircraft. A man without much humour.

"Or bought it," the wireless operator said.

Peter felt their friendliness wash round him, stronger than any difference in living conditions or perquisites of rank. "I jolly nearly made it," he told them. "Got into Holland, but got nabbed by the police. It was my own fault for walking about in broad daylight. What happened to you chaps?"

"Junior didn't get far," Wally said, "did you, Junior?"

Junior grinned. He was a Canadian and the oldest member of the crew. He was lying on one of the lower bunks, both his feet swathed in bandages.

"His boots fell off," Wally explained. "His boots fell off as the parachute opened, and the silly clot walked for two nights in his socks.

"Shucks, I didn't walk very far."

"When they caught him they made him walk seven miles in his socks," Mac said it as a joke.

"The ground was pretty soft though." Junior sighed and wriggled himself more comfortably into the mattress. "I did better than Mac anyway."

Mac had an ugly red cut on his forehead, and one of his

eyes was turning yellow. It had obviously recently been black.

"What on earth happened to you?" Peter asked.

"It wasn't on the — earth," Mac said. "I came down in a — tree. The 'chute got caught in the top branches and left me hanging about fifteen feet from the — ground."

"What did you do, bang the quick-release?"

"My bloody oath—then landed flat on me back."

"That's how you got the black eye!"

"No it — wasn't. I cut my head open as I came down through the branches—but I got the black eye from a silly bastard of a farmer . . . I thought I was in Holland . . ."

There was a hoot of laughter from the listening airmen. "Typical rear-gunner," one of them said. "It's a wonder he didn't think he was over England."

Mac ignored the interruption. "I thought I was in Holland, so I walked up to a farm and asked them for a meal." He looked resentfully at Peter. "What d'you think happened then? The silly bastard hit me in the eye! I sort of realised that I wasn't wanted, and came to the conclusion that I wasn't in Holland after all. He started to scream at me in German so I — off as hard as I could. I'm going back after the war though — I'll get that farmer . . ." Tenderly he stroked his swollen eye. "My bloody oath . . .

"I got into the woods after that, and started to go west. I kept going for a couple of days, and then got picked up by some jokers in green plus fours. I made a dash for it, but they started pooping off shotguns at me. Then I tripped over a root and thought I'd better stay where I — was. How long've you been out of the cooler, Pete?"

"Came out to-day."

"I've got some tucker here." Mac ducked under the clothes-line heavy with damp washing, and crossed to a row of wooden lockers. He returned with a few biscuits and a piece of cheese. "Got these from an Aussie in the cookhouse." The biscuits looked dirty, and the cheese had a semi-circle bitten out of one end, but Peter took them gratefully.

Wally was still stirring his tin on the top of the stove. "Just a minute, Pete—we're making a brew here. Be something to drink with the cheese. Bring me a cup, Teddy."

The engineer handed him two of the large pottery beer mugs from which they had drunk their tea earlier in the morning, and Wally poured out the thick milky liquid.

"What is it?" Peter asked.

"Junior's escape tablets. He managed to get 'em through the search. What sort of time did you have in the cooler, Pete? Did you have a visit from the chap who said he'd shot us down?"

"Yes—he said you told him we were lost."

Wally laughed. "Sorry, Pete, I thought it would save a lot of awkward questions. He got pretty annoyed with me. I told him we were flying an Anson." He handed Peter one of the steaming mugs and, opening the bottom of the stove, raked out half a dozen potatoes which had been roasting there.

"Mac seems to have been pretty busy," Peter said.

" —— Commissariat, that's me!" Mac handed the hot potatoes round among the sergeants. "You've got to have a syndicate in a place like this."

He's ruthless, Peter thought; ruthless and loyal to his group. He could see that Mac would get all there was to get out of captivity, and return to civilian life as hard and ruthless as ever, but more experienced.

"We're being moved to Lamsdorf in a few days," Wally said. "We've all decided to stick together."

"Good show," Peter said. "I haven't heard what's happening to me."

"You'll go to an officers' camp." Mac said it without bitterness. "You look after yourself, Pete—no one else will."

"I'll look after myself," Peter said. "Have you thought about escaping?"

"Not a hope," Mac said. "Lie low till the war's over."

"I'm going to study," Wally said. "Get some good out of it. We're lucky to be alive. Now's the time to catch up and get ready for a job when the war's over." Peter looked at the big, roughly carved head with its mop of unruly hair, and decided that Wally would come through, too. More opinionated perhaps, more humourless, but he'd come through all right.

"Then an old chap with glasses came in," Wally continued, "that was after the chap who said he'd shot us down. This one was an old chap in civilian clothes with a Red Cross badge in his buttonhole. He had a Red Cross form that started off quite normally, asking for your rank, name and number—then went on to ask other things like your squadron and your bomb load. I got as far as rank, name and number and then, when I realised what it was all about I tore the bloody thing up. The old chap was livid—thought he was going to have a fit or something. He didn't look too strong anyway. I made it up to him by telling him that I learned to fly on Tigers."

"Och, I had the same wee fellow." Teddy, the engineer, came from Glasgow. "He asked me if I'd like to broadcast to my people at home, but I told him they hadna got a wireless set."

"Where were you captured?" Peter asked him.

"Och, I hadna got a chance. When I heard the skipper say bale out, I went to get ma parachute. I cuid have sworn I'd left it there on its rack at the rear of the aircraft. But when I got there it wasna there. And it was getting bluidy hot there, in the back of the aircraft. So I thought for a bit, and decided I'd left it by the front escape hatch when I got aboard. I'd meant to bring it up with me but forgot all about it. I scrambled down to where I'd left it, but the flames were right across the aircraft by then and I had to crawl along the floor. There it was, though—balancing on the edge of the open hatch. I cuidna get down there quick enough, I thought it was going to fall out. I cuidna get out quickly enough either—the rest of you had gone hours before, except for Wally yonder and he was sitting there as calm as you like holding her steady. I must have baled out at about five hundred feet, because I knocked myself unconscious, and when I came round there were soldiers standing over me."

Peter turned to Wally to ask the question he had wanted to ask ever since he had entered the room. It still seemed impossible that the pilot could have escaped alive from that burning aircraft. "How in God's name did you get out, Wally?"

"I didn't. I was just thinking of crash-landing when I suddenly saw a lake—so I ditched instead."

"Just like that?"

"I was flying upwind anyway and the lake was pretty big."

"So you just ditched," Peter said. He knew that if it had not been for the lake Wally would never have survived. If it had not been for Wally, sitting there in his blazing aircraft, facing almost certain death so that his crew might escape, none of them would have survived. "So you just ditched," he said, "in the middle of bloody Germany!"

"It wasn't Germany," Wally protested. "It was Holland."

At lunchtime Peter found himself a place next to John Clinton, who was now one of the few men in khaki. The North Africa people had changed their khaki drill for R.A.F. "other ranks" blue serge, and the scene reminded Peter of his early days in Training Command. The conversation was almost entirely of flying, and he felt sympathy for the silent figure by his side. "When did you get caught?" he asked.

"December the seventeenth."

"So was I. How extraordinary. How did they bring you here?"

"By air." The soldier grinned. "It's the only time I've ever flown, I'm afraid."

"Some of these chaps haven't done much more," Peter said. "The more they talk the less they've flown."

"I thought it was rather like that. I always thought it wasn't done to talk about flying in the mess."

"That was the 1914 war. Who's that other Army bod at the head of the table?" The man had intrigued Peter ever since he had entered the room. His face looked as though it had been hacked from red sandstone with a blunt chisel. He had one cauliflower ear, and was dressed in camouflaged paratroop's overalls.

"He's an M.O.," Clinton told him. "He's got a bed in our room. Most extraordinary character. He's brought a bag full of surgical instruments."

"Useful chap to have around. I wonder if he's got any food tablets."

Clinton lowered his voice. "We're thinking about a tunnel from our room. We wondered if you'd be game."

"You can count me in." Peter looked at the doctor eating in silence at the head of the table. He seemed a determined, methodical sort of chap; a man with a certain inflexibility. "He doesn't look much like a doctor," he said.

"He started life as a boxer," Clinton told him, "then he decided he had to be a doctor, so he took his degree. When the war started he was working for a mission in the East End. He's the most gentle creature I've met."

"He looks it."

"No—I mean it. He's so strong that he's gentle with it, like an enormous dog."

When the lunch was over Clinton introduced him to the doctor who suggested a walk round the huts. The man was certainly built like a boxer and walked with a rolling jerk. He had discarded the jumping jacket and was wearing a khaki sweater in which he looked like an American footballer or the hero of a strip cartoon.

He seemed doubtful about the tunnel. "I've been talking to the German M.O.," he explained. "He says that if I put in an application I can be moved to one of the P.O.W. hospitals, on the staff. I'd travel there on my own with one, or possibly two guards. I think I'd have more chance that way than by staying with you chaps. The only thing is that, if I don't make the jump, once I get to the hospital I shall be on parole and unable to escape. I'm rather worried about it. I don't know what to do."

"What about the tunnel from here?" Peter asked.

The doctor laughed. "That's really Clinton's idea. We haven't a hope, really. We haven't time. The German M.O. told me that we'll all be moved in a few days. I think you'd do better by jumping off the train than by digging anyway. A tunnel would take too long."

"We shall have plenty of time where we're going." Clinton said it with surprising bitterness.

"I had a long train journey, coming here," Peter told them. "It's not as easy to jump off a train as you might think. They watch you pretty closely. Besides, even if you got away you'd be in uniform. I'd say you stand a better chance to dig a tunnel from the permanent camp. Get out in the proper clothes and take your time over it."

"I'm not going to a permanent camp," Clinton said. "I must get away before then." He sounded almost desperate.

"Oh, I don't know . . ."

"I must. There are thousands of chaps in permanent camps. Escape will be pretty nearly impossible from there."

"I don't suppose they all try to escape," Peter said. "I've just been talking to some of my crew. They don't even seem to want to get away."

"They will." Clinton was striding at a terrific pace along the beaten path which ran round the compound inside the wire, walking as though he could walk away from his captivity. "They're just numbed now. Most of us are. Now is the time to try to escape. Before it is too late."

"I've been talking to the adjutant again," Peter said. "He still recommends waiting until we get to the permanent camp."

"He should be court-martialled." Clinton was almost running now. "We must strike while the iron is hot."

That evening there was a concert given by the permanent staff in the main dining-hall. Sitting there on the hard wooden form, listening to the competent jazz band, Peter felt that he might have been on any aerodrome in England. There were the same tunes, the same symphonic arrangements of dance numbers, the same sentimental choruses. During the interval there was a free issue of weak German beer, and the second part of the programme was more in the nature of a smoking concert, with "near the knuckle" turns and the community singing of songs, at first nostalgic and sentimental, then bawdy and obscene such as *Salome* and *My Brother Sylveste*. It was a good evening, only spoiled for Peter by a song, composed in the camp and entitled *After The War Is Over*, which by its very defeatism made him realise what they had to fight against.

All one had to do, according to the song, was to wait until the war was over; then "the lights would be bright again," one would be "back in the local," and apparently no one would worry any more.

He left the hut and walked down the floodlit path to his own room, where he found the doctor sewing a scalpel into the hem of his jumping jacket.

"I'm off to-morrow," the doctor said.

"Good luck. Wish I were coming with you."

"You'll get your chance." He looked down at the bag of instruments. "I'm afraid I'll have to leave this lot behind in the train. Anything you'd like out of it?"

Peter chose a couple of the sharpest instruments. He could not imagine how he would use them, but it seemed ungracious to refuse. "I'll take a couple of rolls of bandage, too, if I may—might come in handy. And some Benzedrine tablets, if you've got them. Might want to keep awake some time."

The doctor gave him the bandages and the tablets, and rolled himself up in his blankets. "Must try to get some sleep now."

Peter went to bed, too, but he could not sleep.

When Clinton came in he was mildly drunk. "These R.A.F. chaps aren't so bad, y'know," he said. "I used to think they were a frightful shower."

During the next few days Peter wandered disconsolately round the camp, or chatted with his fellow prisoners. There was a good library in the sergeants' mess, but now that he had the opportunity to read he seemed unable to settle down. It was too impermanent. There was no time in which to plan an escape, yet he felt impelled to walk round and round the camp, looking at the wire. It was fruitless and he knew it. Most of his fellow prisoners seemed to be infected by the same restlessness.

There was a room at the end of their hut, known to the prisoners as the ante-room. It was well furnished and decorated with mural drawings by one of the earlier captives. They were mostly night club and country scenes, the sort of drawing which Peter would hardly have noticed on the walls of a bar in London but which here filled him with unhappy nostalgia.

After breakfast every morning there was a mad rush for the few chairs in the ante-room, and all day long prisoners sat and explained to one another how they had come to be shot down. It became a sort of confessional in which, by talking, they rid themselves of the horror and the sense of failure that had accompanied their capture. It seemed to

G

Peter that they had all narrowly escaped with their lives—
some quietly, almost imperceptibly, as he had done; others
horribly. And they all suffered from reaction in one form
or another, some retiring within themselves, others over-
loud in ante-room debate. Some, mostly the quiet ones,
awoke screaming in the night.

Some of them seemed uncertain of exactly how they had
been shot down. Usually it was a tale of searchlights,
flak, the weaving and rocking of the aircraft, the smell of
burnt cordite, the growing fear; and then the red angry
flames, the black smoke and the sickening jolt of the opening
parachute.

Sometimes it came unexpectedly; the quiet stooging along
miles from the target, the moon and the stars, the flickering
searchlights far away on the horizon, the light-hearted
conversation of the crew. Then, suddenly, there would be
the hammer and din of machine-gun bullets, or the heavier,
tearing impact of cannon shells, as a night-fighter closed in
from behind them. Sometimes they would fight back.
More often than not they would plunge towards the earth,
spinning and screaming through the air, a great wake of
fire and smoke following them down.

Always there was the sudden losing of fear in the face of
danger, the quiet acceptance of what was to come, and the
queer surprise and relief at finding oneself on the ground
and away from the fire and the batter and crash of the shells.

Not all the men had come down by parachute. Some had
landed in their blazing aircraft, to be thrown out on impact
with the ground. Some had been dragged from the flames
by their comrades; others had been saved by friendly
German soldiers. One man had come down, from seven
thousand feet, hanging by one foot from his parachute
harness. Another, a navigator, had been held in his seat by
centrifugal force while the aircraft hurtled towards the
ground. Then the aircraft had disintegrated in mid air, and
he had been thrown clear, retaining enough consciousness

to pull the ripcord before he fainted. He woke up lying in a ploughed field, half his flying clothes burned away, but otherwise unhurt.

It was here, at *Dulag-Luft*, that Peter wrote his first letter home; a letter that was difficult to write, as he could not say anything about how he came to be where he was, nor anything about his captors. He asked for warm under-clothes and wrote down a tangle of platitudes and veiled references from which he hoped his mother would be able to unravel enough to set her mind at rest. He also wrote to Roy telling him that the crew had agreed that he should have the car.

A few days later the sergeants left for Lamsdorf. Standing in the slush of the compound, watching them march away, he felt that his last link with the world he knew was being broken. He turned back into the camp, but could not face the crowded ante-room. It was all so mean, so sordid; squabbling over who was to have the slightly larger slice of bread, bolting breakfast to rush and bag a chair; queuing early in order to get the best seat at the concert. It was infectious, he was doing it himself. It was like it had been when he first joined up; a crowd of adults thrown together, without common loyalties nor ties of any sort. Later, when they had started on the navigation course, there had been the common goal of the "Wings" exam, but here they had nothing. Not even the remote aim of trying to win the war. The future was grey and endless; endless feeble chatter, endless preoccupation with rations, endless lack of privacy. He thrust his hands deep into his trouser pockets and plodded slowly round the wire, head down, shoulders hunched; a typical forlorn "kriegie" attitude.

That evening he heard that the paratroop doctor had been killed while jumping off the train on his way to the hospital at Obermassfeld.

CHAPTER VI

EVERY WEEK a list of names of those who were to be
"purged" to a permanent camp was pinned to the
notice-board in the dining-room. This week the purge was
to *Oflag XXIB* in Poland, and Peter's name was in the list.
He was glad to see that John Clinton was going with him.
There was something about the young Army officer's quiet
self-sufficiency that had captured his respect. He had
shaken off the first, almost panic-stricken frenzy to get away
and spent most of his time reading. It seemed a complete
reversal of his earlier frame of mind, but Peter sensed that
he was holding himself firmly in check, realising that their
stay in this transit camp was short, tiding over the time
until he could concentrate wholly on the problem of escape.

As soon as Peter knew that at last they were really going,
he began to make plans for his own escape. The dark night
hours spent wrestling with the shame of capture had
hardened his early misery into a cold resolve. Convinced
that he had not made the most of his opportunities, refusing
to accept excuses from himself, he vowed that he too would
make his getaway.

He sewed special hidden pockets into the lining of his
greatcoat, where he concealed the scalpels and the little food
he had managed to collect. He spent hours in the library
studying an encyclopædia from which the censor had
omitted to remove the maps. He traced some of the maps
on to toilet paper and hid them with the other things. But
the doctor's death had made him even more pessimistic
about jumping trains, and he knew in his heart that this
preparation was merely a front to convince himself that
he was doing all he could to get away.

At last the purge party was assembled outside the huts, complete with baggage. Peter was amazed at the quantity some of them had managed to collect in so short a time. They were made to march to the station, which was several miles away, and he was glad that he had decided to travel light.

John Clinton carried his luggage in his pockets, including a book that he had taken from the prison library. He marched with an amused expression in his eyes.

"What's so funny?" Peter asked.

"These chaps with their bundles. They look like the lost tribes of Israel."

"Maybe they've got some sense. You don't know where we might find ourselves." Peter shifted his small bundle from one shoulder to the other. "Probably just as well to have something to start life with. It may be a perfectly new camp, with nothing there at all."

"There's no point in preparing to settle down," Clinton muttered. "If you set out with that idea you'll never get away. Look at that chap!" He nodded towards a broad, stocky air-gunner named Saunders, who was staggering along under the burden of an unwieldy bundle wrapped in a blanket. He had a large "Bomber Command" moustache, and wore a balaclava helmet and flying boots.

"Old Bill looking for a better 'ole," Peter said. "I wonder what he's got in the bundle."

"Doesn't matter what it is. It shows that he's preparing to settle down."

At the railway station they were lined up by the *Feldwebel* and then addressed by the officer in charge. "Gentlemen," he said, "you will be some days in the train. If you behave reasonably, you will be reasonably treated. If you attempt to escape, you will be shot. This is not an idle threat. The guards have been given instructions to shoot any prisoner who attempts to escape. There is a live round in every barrel. That is all, gentlemen."

They were herded into carriages which were divided into compartments in the English fashion, but the seats were wooden. Peter found himself squeezed into the corner of a compartment opposite a tall fair flight lieutenant and Saunders, who had arrived triumphant with his bundle, which he put on the floor between their legs. Next to Peter sat Clinton, already reading his book.

"Any more for Margate?" Saunders seemed determined to make it a pleasant journey. He handed cigarettes round, and soon the air was thick and stale with smoke. Four men at the far end of the compartment began a game of cards. Peter wondered which of them had been shot down with a pack of playing cards in his pocket—or had he picked them up at *Dulag-Luft*? Saunders had evidently been laying in a stock of something or other, judging by the size of his bundle. Peter looked at him closely. A red good-humoured face with a mouth that smiled easily under his grotesque moustache, a smile that was half-suppressed like that of a schoolboy. The mass of untidy hair, tow-coloured, and a quick dogmatic way of speaking that was not aggressive. An easy chap to get along with.

The flight lieutenant was of a different breed. Fair and slim, even in his issue uniform he looked immaculate; his moustache was short and carefully tended. His name was Hugo, and he sat now as though the whole trip had been arranged as a sort of pleasure outing in which, although not entirely approving, he felt he ought to play his part.

Two hours later the train was still in the station. They had made several false starts, but had been shunted back to their original position again. At last, as though satisfied with the lesson it had taught them, the engine whistled in derision, and slowly the train pulled out.

Long hours of sitting on a wooden seat . . . nothing to

read . . . falling asleep, and waking stiff . . . smoking, yawning, and moving restlessly . . . thinking of home . . .

Often the train stopped for no apparent reason, miles from any station. Each time it stopped, the German soldiers jumped down on to the track, and stood with tommy-guns at the ready until it started again. Each time it stopped, Peter tensed himself to escape, but each time he saw that it was hopeless. There were raised sentry boxes, fitted with machine-guns, at both ends of every carriage.

. . . Long hours of standing still on railway stations, with the curious public peering in as though at animals . . . stiffness and soreness . . . hunger and thirst . . . the agony of knowing that outside the carriage window the country-side stretched golden in the winter sunshine . . . occasion-ally a placid canal or tumbling stream . . . knowing it, but not being able to see it because the window was steamed up . . . knowing that there were wide rivers, with steamers and strings of brightly-coloured barges with peasant women at their tillers . . . knowing it only by the hollow sound made by the train as it crossed the bridge . . .

. . . Twelve men in one compartment, and only one man allowed by the guards to stand at a time . . . ten minutes' standing, and two hours' sitting in agony on a wooden seat . . . wanting desperately to stand and stretch, but sitting, willing the time to pass . . . talk, talk, talk. . . .

John Clinton, when he had finished with his book, which was of no use to the others as it was Latin verse, proved himself a lively and interesting travelling companion. He told them that he had been born in Malaya, that his father owned a rubber plantation where he had lived until he was sent home to school in England. He had just gone up to Oxford when the war started, and he had joined the Army. He kept them amused for hours with stories of his batman, who had watched him like a hawk to see that he changed his socks and underclothes, dosed him with laxatives that he did not need and wrote a weekly bulletin to his mother reporting on his health and spirits. At intervals his mother would get a letter beginning, "Madam you will be pleased to hear that we have received further promotion and are now captain . . ." or, "Madam our shirts are becoming a little worn . . ." Clinton had enjoyed his life in the Army and spoke with humour and warmth of his troop of bren-gun carriers. It seemed to Peter that if he needed a partner in his escape he could go a long way and not find a better man than John Clinton.

Saunders, who together with his brother ran a green-grocer's shop in North London, did not appear disturbed at the prospect of several years' captivity. The business would go on and in time he would return to it. He took life as it came, finding it good and full of queer incidents which he invited the others to observe from his own original and slightly derisive viewpoint. Life to him, too, was something to be chuckled at, a chuckle in his case at once suppressed and followed by a quick look over his shoulder. He had started his career with a kerbside barrow off Oxford Street, and still retained that furtive, quick look round for the police.

Hugo on the other hand seemed almost devoid of humour. He was gentle, languid and charmingly self-centred. He made a perfect foil for Saunders. His main concerns at the moment were that there would be no facilities for washing in the camp—as, indeed, there were none on the train—and that he would not be given enough to eat. "What couldn't I do to a steak," he sighed. "With lashings of chip potatoes and red gravy. A T-bone steak."

"I'd settle for a plate of fish and chips," Saunders said.

"I'd settle for a tin of spam," Peter added.

"All you chaps think about is food," John said. "When I was in the desert——"

"Look out," Saunders said. "There's that sand blowing in again!"

But for the most of the time the four men were silent, trying to sleep or quiet with their thoughts. From the rest of the compartment Peter heard snatches of bored, unlistened to, repeated anecdote.

"——stooged straight up Happy Valley. The flak was so thick that it looked like Piccadilly in peacetime."

"I reckon there'll be bags of opportunity to study. Might take a degree of some sort. Law or accountancy."

"——turned on E.T.A., came down through the cloud, and there I was—smack over——"

"I'm going to settle down. A nice little pub in Devonshire——"

"——came down so fast that the altimeter stuck."

"I reckon we shall be allowed out for walks. In the last war——"

"Take coalmining, one of the dirtiest jobs on the face of the earth——"

"——go out disguised as a German. All you need is a uniform and the right papers. Speaking German is an advantage, of course."

"——her husband was a commercial traveller——"

"——used to fly by the seat of his pants."

"Yes, but that's capitalism in a way——"

"——best ride I ever had——"

"But it says so in the Geneva Convention—so long as you're in uniform——"

Recollection, explanation, rationalisation, speculation . . .

Beyond the steamed-up window miles and miles of pine forest, dark inside but with the tall trunks of the outer trees reddened by the sun; inside the compartment boredom and depression, hunger and thirst, the smell of old socks, the choky heaviness of the smoke-filled atmosphere.

Then the failure of the heating plant, the cold.

The cold.

Icicles, formed by their breath on the window-pane—breaking them off to suck because they had no water.

By the third day they had eaten their rations and Peter had given up all hope of escape from the train. He took the food that he had saved from the hidden pockets in his coat, and shared it round among the men at his end of the compartment. Following his example, John Clinton produced a hidden store of food which he too shared. "Might as well eat it as let the Germans have it," he said. They looked at the others expectantly, but apparently any plans they had made to escape did not include a stock of food.

Late in the afternoon of the fourth day the train made one of its customary halts at a small wayside station, but this time it was different. The escort came down the train, shouting, "'*Raus, 'raus! Ausgehen, alle ausgehen!*"

Looking out of the open door Peter saw that they had been surrounded by a cordon of soldiers, steel-helmeted and armed with tommy-guns.

"This is it," Saunders said. "Full military honours, too."

It was growing dark as they got down from the train. A fine sleet was falling, powdering their greatcoats and restricting their view. It was colder here than it had been in Frankfurt, and as far as Peter could see there was nothing but a flat unbroken sheet of snow. "Looks as though we've come to Siberia," Saunders said.

There were arc lamps hanging by the side of the track and the prisoners were paraded there for roll-call. They were counted three times before the guards could find the correct number and they were able to set out, at a shambling gait, for the camp.

The road led them straight across a plain towards a village whose few pale lights flickered wanly through the falling snow. It was little more than a track, seamed and furrowed by passing carts but improving as it neared the village, until they were marching on cobblestones which rang under the steel of their boots. The guards—there were nearly as many guards as there were prisoners—marched at their side, tommy-guns at the ready, while in front and behind the column were lorries with searchlights and machine-guns.

As they neared the village, some of the men at the head of the column began to sing. Slowly the song crept down the ranks until the whole company was singing. To Peter, walking in embarrassed silence, it seemed that they were singing to show the villagers that, although captured, they were not defeated; he was thankful that they had chosen, not a patriotic song, but *Bless 'Em All* as their tune.

Leaving the village behind them they climbed a long hill, stumbling and slipping on the icy road. They were tired now, and had stopped singing. Presently they saw the lights of the camp ahead, the great circle of arc lamps, and the searchlights sweeping slowly across the empty compound. As they drew near a searchlight was turned on them, blinding them and throwing long shadows from the unevenness of the snow-packed road. It lit up their pale faces, dark beginnings of beards, the odd shape of scarves tied round their heads and the bundles they carried on their backs.

The gates were thrown open and the long straggling line of prisoners marched into the camp, peering through the darkness for some hint of what they were to expect. They could only see the wire, bright and hard in the light of the arc lamps, and the black and red-striped sentry box. Untidily they closed up on the leading ranks, who had halted. The gates were shut behind them with a creak and clatter of chains.

The prisoners eased the bundles from their shoulders. Some of them lit cigarettes; a *Feldwebel* ran up and down the column telling them not to smoke, but they took no notice. The falling snow settled on their heads and shoulders as they stood waiting in the horizontal beam of the search-light.

Then they were counted again, several times. Peter heard the Germans arguing about the count, and was filled with a feeling of sick futility. He stood in the cold muddy snow of the compound dumbly waiting for the guards to make a move. All he wanted was to get out of the snow. He thought with nostalgia of the dry room at *Dulag-Luft*. Even the railway carriage would have been better than this.

At last the guards agreed on the count, and the prisoners were marched into a large cement-faced building which stood just beyond the light of the arc lamps.

As he stood in the long queue, Peter wondered why they must be searched again. They had been searched before leaving *Dulag-Luft;* what could the Germans imagine they would have picked up during the journey? When his turn came, he stood and watched the guard trying to unravel the series of elaborate knots with which he had tied his bundle —the Germans never used knives, too salvage-conscious, he supposed. He wished he had added a few more knots for luck. The things the doctor had given him, together with the small brass compass and the maps he had copied from the encyclopædia were safe in their hidden pockets, and he managed to get them through undiscovered.

When the last man had been searched the prisoners were taken to a large hall, where they were handed over to the Senior British Officer. There were tables and forms set out in the hall, and the newcomers were given a cup of tea and two slices of black bread thinly spread with jam. When they had eaten they were addressed by the tall lean group captain, whose lined face looked haggard under his battered service cap.

"Gentlemen," he said, "before you go to your new quarters

I should like to say a few words about the general running of this camp. The organisation is simple, and I want to keep it that way. I, as Senior British Officer, am responsible to the German authorities for all that goes on inside the camp; but I'll tell you more about that later.

"The building you are in is known as the White House. It was once a reformatory, but no prisoners sleep here now. It is used for the camp theatre and lecture rooms and for the library. Normally no prisoners are allowed in the building after dark.

"There are ten barrack blocks in the compound. Each barrack block is divided into twelve messes. In each mess there are eight officers. Each barrack block is under the command of a wing commander or a squadron leader. Each mess has a senior officer, who is responsible to the block commander for the conduct of his mess.

"All discipline is self-imposed. You will find, before you have been very long in the camp, that most of our energy is devoted to a ceaseless war against the enemy. To carry on this war, a spirit of loyalty and service is essential. You will find such a spirit in this camp.

"Our foremost activity is—escape. Do not forget that there are men here who have been escaping ever since they were captured. At the moment there is a tunnel half-way towards the wire. No—don't be alarmed. I can speak freely. The guards have gone, and we have stooges posted at every window. I tell you this because I want to warn you against ill-considered attempts at escape. If you rashly take the first chance that offers itself, it is more than likely that you will fail. That is not important; what is important is that, in failing, you may uncover another, long-planned scheme that, but for your interference, might have succeeded.

"There is a special body of officers in this camp known as the Escape Committee. It is their job to co-ordinate and assist all escape attempts. If you have an idea, take it to them. Do not be afraid that by doing so you will lose control of the scheme. It is your scheme, and you will be the first man to leave the camp by means of it, if it succeeds. The Escape Committee will arrange for your forged passports and civilian clothes. We have special departments whose only job is making these things. If you have a scheme of escape, take it to the Committee. They are all experienced men, and they will give you all the help they can.

"The Germans have their own security branch. It is known as the *Abwehr*. They employ specially trained men we call 'ferrets.' You will recognise them in the camp by their blue overalls and the long steel spikes they carry. These men are dangerous. They all speak English and are expert in the discovery of escape activity. You will find them hiding under the floor and in the roof, listening at the keyhole and the windows. Look out for them.

"We have our counter-ferrets. We call them 'stooges.' Every ferret that comes into the camp is shadowed by a stooge. There are stooges standing at every window and door as I am talking. Before I began, they searched every possible hiding-place within hearing distance of this room. You, also, will be asked to volunteer for this duty. It is practically the only duty you will be asked to perform, and I hope you will do it cheerfully.

"If you attempt to escape—and I hope you will—you will find it an ungrateful task. Its greatest function is that it boosts the morale of your fellow prisoners. They feel that while there is an escape attempt in operation we are doing something against the enemy—not just vegetating. As I told you when we first met, there is a wonderful spirit in this camp. I hope that you will foster that spirit."

When the group captain had gone, the new purge was divided into groups to be distributed among the ten barrack blocks. Peter and John Clinton made up a party with Saunders, the air-gunner, and Hugo, the tall immaculate flight lieutenant.

As they made their way down the stairs of the White House Peter felt the warmth and integrity of the group captain still with him. Here was a man to follow, a man with something positive to offer. What a difference between this and the weak opportunism of *Dulag-Luft*. He was almost cheerful again, eager to take his part in the war that would continue in this camp.

Outside, it was still snowing. The roofs of the barrack blocks were covered in snow, but the ground inside the compound had been churned into thick black sludge. Duckboard rafts outside the doors of the long low barracks were half under water, and the newcomers cursed as they squelched their way through the darkness.

The door to their barrack block was secured by lock and bar—a modern lock, Peter noticed, and a wooden bar four inches thick, resting in heavy iron brackets. The guard unfastened the door and led them into a small vestibule. The by now familiar stench, which had so astonished them during their first days at *Dulag-Luft*, told them what lay beyond the door which faced them—typical German P.O.W. sanitation.

There were two more double doors on their right, and these the guard kicked open without ceremony.

After the freshness of the night, the fug inside was over-powering. The big low room was almost in darkness. Through the gloom of smoke and steam, Peter could see row upon row of two-tier wooden bunks diminishing into hazy perspective. As his eyes grew accustomed to the smoke he noticed that the bunks had been pulled out from the walls to form a series of small rooms. In each room stood a wooden table on which a guttering home-made lamp shed a feeble dull red glow. Smoke from these lamps joined with steam from rows and rows of damp washing which hung on lines almost down to head level, to form clouds which billowed and eddied under the roof. The concrete floor was puddled with the water which dripped incessantly

from the rows of washing. There were windows in each of
the side walls, but these were covered from the outside by
black-out shutters. There seemed to be no ventilation
whatever.

Round each small table sat a group of prisoners playing
cards or trying to read by the light of the home-made
lamps, which threw weird and distorted shadows on the
walls, once whitewashed, now grey and smeared by smoke
and steam. Most of the men were wearing beards, their hair
was long, and they shuffled round in wooden clogs or sat
huddled on their bunks, blankets hunched round their
shoulders, merging with the shadows that surrounded
every feeble light. There was a buzz of conversation which
dropped into curious silence as the new arrivals entered.

In one corner of the room a reedy gramophone ground out
a dance tune, strident in the sudden hush.

A figure emerged from the shadows and came towards
them. He was wearing a worn R.A.F. tunic on which,
below the pilot's wings, was the ribbon of the D.F.C. with
bar. On the sleeves, almost worn away, were the three
rings of a wing commander. He was dark and bearded,
and his feet were thrust into huge wooden clogs which he
scraped along the concrete floor as he walked.

"Hallo, chaps—are you the new lot from *Dulag*?"

"Yes, sir."

"Good show. Sorry about the light—it'll come on again
presently, I expect. Bloody goon reprisal. My name's
Stewart. Had a rough journey?"

"Pretty grim, sir, yes."

"Well, we've got some food fixed up for you. And by
the way, don't call me ' sir '—we dispense with that sort of
thing here. You'll want a wash before you eat. Just drop
your things, and I'll show you round. You've got soap
and towels, I expect."

He took them down the central gangway formed by
narrow wooden lockers, which screened off the "rooms"

which lay behind them. "You'll find us a bit bolshie, I expect, but the morale is pretty good—the Hun can't do a thing with us."

Peter, glancing in through the narrow doorways between the lockers, saw that the messes were divided one from the other by bunks standing at right angles to the wall. Each mess had a table and two long wooden forms, and seemed isolated, drawn round its own centre of fitful light. The effect of a squalid prolific slum was intensified by the festoons of washing which hung everywhere.

As they entered the washroom at the far end of the block, the electric light came on. There was a round of ironic cheers from the prisoners in the larger room.

"It won't be for long," Stewart told them. "The goons do it for fun. You'd better take advantage of it and get washed up while you can."

Peter looked at the two long cement troughs, above which ran an iron pipe with taps at intervals. There were wooden duck-boards on the floor, which was awash with greasy water. "The drains have stopped up again," Stewart explained. "We complain about it every day, but it doesn't do any good."

The newcomers set about removing some of the accumulated dirt of the four days' journey. The water was cold. As Peter washed, he thought of the wing commander's description "bolshie." What did he mean by bolshie? The place was certainly primitive enough. He looked round him at the flooded floor and dirty walls.

There was a sudden burst of conversation and loud laughter from the large room, as the door opened and a man came out carrying a large tin which he began to fill under one of the taps. He was dressed in a short sleeveless jacket roughly cobbled from blankets. His hair was cropped down to a quarter of an inch in length, and as he waited for the tin to fill he sang softly to himself. Peter watched him furtively; it seemed almost unbelievable that this

H

could be a British officer. He felt as he had felt on his first day at school. When the man had gone, he looked across the trough at John, who was washing his beard. "What d'you make of this?" he asked.

"Better than the last place," John said. "It's got a sort of discipline. You know where you are, in a place like this."

"Looks pretty grim to me." Hugo ran a wet comb through his hair, patting the wave into shape with his hand. "Almost a boy scout atmosphere."

"It'll be all right." Saunders was holding his dental plate under the running tap. Without his teeth his face looked old and drawn. "Better than the flak over Duisburg, any road."

"I didn't mind the flak." Hugo was now combing his moustache. "You can put up with almost anything if you've got civilised living conditions."

"Listen to him," Saunders said. "Civilised living conditions! He doesn't know he's alive." To Hugo, "I bet you've never been hungry in your life."

"Not until I came to Germany."

"Then you've been lucky," Saunders told him.

The wing commander called them together. Under the shadow of his beard his face was thin. "I know you've just had a pi-jaw from the S.B.O., so I'll make mine as short as possible. I'm going to put you chaps in the end mess, but for dinner this evening you will each go to a different mess, partly because we've drawn no rations for you yet and partly"—he grinned—"so that you can give all the gen about home. You're the first batch from England since we arrived here, so you'll have to answer a lot of questions. Do it as cheerfully as you can—the chaps have been away a long time.

"Flight Lieutenant Tyson is the hut representative on the Escape Committee, and if you want to escape we'll give you all the help we can. Your chances of getting back are practically nil. I'm telling you this because we don't want the game cluttered up with chaps who aren't prepared to put in everything they've got.

"Another thing: Don't be polite to the Hun. Don't let him be polite to you. If we behaved ourselves he could do with a tenth of the number of guards he has to use now. Relax for a moment, say a polite word to him—and you'll find yourself becoming a dead-beat. Don't forget for a single second that these are your enemies. Do everything in your power to make their job as difficult as you can.

"I'm putting you in the end mess. There's a chap there you might find a bit of a strain at first, he's a queer type. But there will only be six of you instead of the usual eight. You should be able to cope. Stick it as long as you can anyway, and if you find it too much let me know."

"What d'you mean," Saunders asked, "a queer type?"

"Oh, he's a bit round the bend, that's all. Strain, y'know. There's a Pole, too; his name's Otto Sechevitsky. He more or less looks after Loveday. If I were you I'd be guided by Otto until you know the ropes. You'll find life a bit strange here at first no doubt, and Otto's got the thing buttoned up as well as anybody. If you follow him you won't go far wrong."

He took them to a mess at the extreme end of the block, near the entrance and unpleasantly close to the latrine.

Otto and Loveday were playing chess. The wing commander introduced them. "I'll leave you now," he said. "Otto will look after you."

As soon as he had gone, Loveday rose to his feet. He was a tall raw-boned man and his nose looked as though it had been squashed in below his protuberant forehead. The eyes, deep-set, slanted upwards and outwards, giving the face a cunning look belied by the wide slack mouth which showed red and moist through the tangled beard. He was wearing clogs, a greatcoat and a Balaclava helmet.

He cleared his throat. "*I'll* look after you individuals. You are all suffering from shock. You are all a bit unstrung.

But I understand the position." He spoke slowly, punctuating each word with a stabbing movement of one of his large raw-looking hands. "I make allowances for newcomers. It's fate that sent you here. And fate that sent me to look after you. Ain't that right, Otter?" He chuckled without mirth and looked at Otto, who smiled in an embarrassed way. "You may think an individual has free will—but he hasn't. Life's a chess-board and we're all pawns." He knocked one of the pieces from the board with a sweep of his mittened right hand and looked at Peter. "Ain't that right?" he said.

Peter hesitated. "Er—yes," he said.

Loveday looked at him for a long time, while Peter felt himself colour with confusion.

"You'll learn," Loveday said. "You'll learn soon enough. Won't he, Otter? He'll learn in time." He looked round at the others. "You'll all learn." He looked at the chess-board and chuckled again. "Little pawns on a big board." He began to drum his fingers on the table-top.

"All the bunks are free," Otto said, "except these two." He indicated the two-tier wooden bedstead farthest from the doorway. He was a thin brittle-looking man whose grey eyes were calm and patient beneath a mass of straw-coloured hair. He looked oddly military and neat standing there beside Loveday's untidy bulk. "Just put your things down and I'll make some tea. The other chaps will call for you when they want to take you to dinner."

Dinner. Peter's stomach contracted and he felt a sudden spasm of nausea. Dinner. He had not eaten a hot meal since leaving *Dulag-Luft*. He hoped that they would not be too long before they called for him.

On each bunk was a sack filled with wood shavings, as a mattress, and a smaller sack, as a pillow. There were thin shoddy blankets, and two sheets and a pillowcase of coarse cotton. He chose the bunk above the one that John had chosen, leaving Hugo to share with Saunders. Loveday watched them as they unpacked.

"I can see you individuals are not used to this sort of thing," he said. "You have come straight from your comfortable homes and you're bound to be upset. You're suffering from shock. Everybody in the camp is suffering from shock. Eh, Otter?"

Otto smiled. "O.K., Alan—so we all suffer from shock. Let us forget it. I will make tea." He took a packet of tea from a shelf, put half of it in a large metal jug and walked out of the mess.

Peter began to arrange his few possessions on the rough shelf which the previous owner had fixed above his bunk. All his early enthusiasm had collapsed before the impact of this overcrowded slum. How could one escape, submerged beneath this turmoil? The room was loud with the roar and chatter of a hundred voices, filled with the bustle of a hundred different aims. He worked in silence, conscious of the tall figure of Alan Loveday watching them unpack.

"I've got a book here." Loveday took down a large book from the shelf above his bunk. "It tells you how to handle people. An individual has to know how to handle people in a place like this."

Peter looked down at John and raised his eyebrows.

"What's the book called?" John asked.

"*A Textbook of Psychology*. Psychology is the study of the mind. This is a good place to study psychology, because everybody is suffering from shock. Everybody is a bit abnormal round here."

"Yes," John said. "I suppose you're right."

"I don't need you to tell me when I'm right," Loveday shouted. "I'm telling *you*!" He glared angrily at John. "Just because you talk with an Oxford accent is no reason for you to tell me when I'm right!"

John was silent.

"This is a different world from the one you've lived in," Loveday continued. He was standing on one foot, the other resting on a stool at the end of the table. His mittened hands plucked restlessly at his beard. "This is a world where you have to study other individuals. Things are not the same here. Everybody——"

"Goon in the block!" It was one of the prisoners at the far end of the barrack. Soon the chanted cry was taken up on all sides. "Goon in the block! Goon in the block!"

"What's that?" Peter asked.

"It's the German guards doing the rounds," Loveday explained. "The other chaps always call out when they come in. It's a sort of warning. I always ignore them myself. When an individual . . ."

Peter went to the doorway of the mess, and looked down the central corridor. Followed by the jeers and catcalls of the prisoners, the tall, heavily-built guard walked down the centre of the barrack block, with his dog, a big Alsatian, on a chain.

"Two goons approaching," someone called, "one leading the other!"

The guard, ponderous in his heavy jackboots and his long green greatcoat girdled by a thick, unpolished leather belt, walked slowly down the corridor, the dog slavering and straining at the leash.

"What do they do that for?" Peter asked.

Loveday laughed. "It's psychological. They do it to frighten us. They turn the dogs loose in the compound every night. They're trained to savage everyone except the owner. One man to one dog. No one else can handle them."

CHAPTER VII

PETER WAS collected for dinner by a flight lieutenant who introduced himself as Tyson. He went willingly, Loveday's insistent voice ringing in his ears.

"Loveday been holding forth already?" Tyson was a tall man with a big jaw and a pleasant voice. He wore a black high-necked sweater under his service tunic, and strode quickly over the damp concrete floor in leather flying boots. "You mustn't mind him—he's a bit round the bend, that's all."

"Round the bend?"

"Oh—wire fever. It comes in waves. Some chaps get it worse than others. With some it's acute depression, others definitely get a little queer. It's different with Loveday, though. I reckon he was a mental case before he was captured."

"You mean, he's always like that?"

"More or less. He's never violent, you know. He's been in every mess in the block so far. No one can stand him for long."

"Poor devil." Peter could imagine him, friendless, pushed round from mess to mess.

"Oh, he's happy enough. Happier than a lot of us, I should think. It's you I'm sorry for. Here we are!" He led the way into a mess in which three men were sitting at the table. They looked as though they had been waiting for him to arrive.

"This is Flight Lieutenant Howard," Tyson said. "Commander Drew, Flight Lieutenant Crawford, Lieutenant Simpson. The others are getting dinner ready." He motioned Peter to a seat at the head of the table. "Will you have a drink?"

Peter must have shown his surprise, because they all laughed.

"No whisky or anything like that," the commander said hastily. "It's a little brew we make from raisins. We keep it for special occasions." He poured five small tots of colourless liquid from a tin into five large pottery mugs. "Forgive the glasses—they're all we have at the moment."

The brew was strong, it tasted like petrol. Peter was glad the tot had been a small one.

"Now, how long do you think the war will last?" The commander, leaning across the table, spoke as though he were asking what would win the Derby—for a hot tip. He was big and gruff, and his blue eyes were set in laughter-lines above his wide, aggressively-curling beard.

Peter thought quickly. He hadn't the faintest idea how long the war would last. They obviously wanted to be reassured. "I give it a year," he said.

"Ah!" the commander sighed, and leaned back as though a great weight had been lifted from his mind. "That's my impression, too."

"I'd give it longer than that," Crawford said. He was an older man than the others, and he had an anxious, almost fretful look. He wore a long khaki overcoat, spoils of some forgotten army, and his knitted woollen cap was pulled low down around his ears. "We've got to get our full bombing force into operation," he explained. "We're only playing at it so far. Yes—I give it two years at least. Possibly two-and-a-half."

"Nonsense, Tom!" The commander smiled at Peter. "You'll never win a war by bombing."

Simpson, who was younger than the others and wore the navy blue battledress of the Fleet Air Arm, held out a packet of cigarettes and offered Peter a light from a small lamp which was burning on the table, a round tobacco tin containing liquid fat. A metal bridge had been made across the open top of the tin, and through this bridge was threaded a woollen wick which burned with a small blue flame. "It's almost impossible to get matches here," Simpson explained, "so we keep a permanent light. What's the latest show in Town?"

As Peter lit the cigarette he tried to remember. He hadn't seen a show in the West End since he joined the squadron. "*Blithe Spirit*'s a good show," he hazarded.

The commander snorted. "That was on before I was shot down. That was old when Pontius was a pilot!"

Peter thought again. "There's a very good show at the Windmill," he said, "but I can't remember its name. I'm afraid I'm not very well up in that sort of thing."

"What were you flying?" Tyson asked.

Peter felt safer here. "Stirlings," he said. "I started on Wimpeys and we converted on to Stirlings. I only did about five trips in Stirlings, and most of those were over Italy."

"Lousy kites, Stirlings." Crawford was obviously a reactionary. "Wouldn't be seen dead in one. Give me a Wimpey any day. What was the Italian flak like?"

"Piece of cake," Peter told him. "They haven't a clue. We used to stooge around watching the fires."

"Where were you shot down?"

"Over Germany. A night-fighter got us, chased us down to the deck and then set us on fire . . ." He was just getting started when the other members of the mess arrived with dinner. There were three of them and each seemed to be carrying something.

The commander attempted to continue the conversation but it was obvious that he was more interested in the meal than he was in flying over Italy. "The equipment's a bit primitive, I'm afraid," he said, indicating the seven pottery bowls, like pudding basins, which the others had set out on the bedsheet-covered table. "But we've got the best cook in the block—eh, Jonah?"

"We've got the biggest appetite," Jonah said. He was a plump Canadian and apparently treated his cooking with all the seriousness due to that high art. There were tinned sausages, tinned tomatoes, fried potatoes and Smedley's peas; all hot and arranged in attractive symmetry on a large roughly-constructed tray. On closer inspection Peter saw that the tray was made from dozens of small pieces of tin beaten flat and joined with folded seams.

Jonah hovered, reluctant to break up his artistic arrangement and put the food into the thick pottery bowls.

"Double up, Jonah!" The commander had taken his seat at the head of the table and was impatiently smoothing his beard.

Peter was seated at the commander's right hand. "Do you have a separate cook for every mess?" he asked.

"Yes, we all mess separately." The commander attacked his food with vigour. "In most messes they take it in turns to be cook. We're jolly lucky in old Jonah, he likes cooking and takes it all off our shoulders. We give him a hand with the potato peeling and the washing up."

"It's the only way I can get a decent meal," Jonah explained.

Peter's heart sank; he had never cooked anything more complicated than a boiled egg in his life. He hoped fervently that one of his mess would prove as great a gourmet as Jonah.

"Do you have a meal like this every night?" he asked.

The commander smiled. "No, I think Jonah's surpassed himself this evening. Each mess gets four Red Cross parcels a week. We usually manage one hot meal a day, but not as good as this. The other meals we make out with bread. Some chaps get used to it but I must admit I'm always hungry." He sighed.

As he ate Peter noticed the tactful manner of these older prisoners, the consideration with which they treated one another. They had obviously come to grips with their imprisonment and forced it to become as gracious as circumstances would allow. He remembered the frantic scrambling and pushing at *Dulag-Luft*, and wondered if these men had ever been like that. They were so quiet, with a calm reserve that made him feel soft and ineffective. He sensed that their disapproval would be a cutting and permanent thing.

After dinner they sat round the table drinking Nescafé out of the mugs which had contained the "brew" and asked him questions about home; questions that he found difficult to answer. If only I'd known I was going to be shot down, he thought. I'd have got all the dope ready. He managed to give them the current prices of beer and whisky, but when they asked him about food rationing and other topical news he realised his total inadequacy.

"What's the cigarette position?" Simpson asked.

"Pretty grim at the moment," Peter said. "Tobacconists keep a few under the counter, but unless they know you it's pretty difficult. I've been to half a dozen shops running before now and not been able to buy any."

"That's one good thing about this place," the commander said. "We get more cigarettes than we can smoke. They're the only thing one's friends can send out in any quantity they like. They're not allowed to send food, so they all send cigarettes. Would you like some?"

"I smoke a pipe myself," Peter said. "But I'll take some for the others if I may."

The commander got up and went over to his locker. "Here's two hundred," he said, "and four ounces of Capstan. Let me know when you get short."

"Thanks very much, that's grand." Peter made a neat pile of the cigarette packets on the table and put the tobacco tins beside them. "Things don't seem so bad as I'd thought at first . . ."

The commander smiled. "We've got a financial wizard in our mess. He was on the Stock Exchange before the war, and now he works a racket on the food market every morning."

Peter did not understand.

"You'll see the market to-morrow," the commander told him. "It's in a little hut down by the White House. It's worked on a system of points. Supposing you get a clothing parcel from home, and there's something in it you don't want. Well, instead of trying to exchange it for something somebody else doesn't want, you go down to the mart and pop it. You get so many points for it, which you can either spend then and there or have entered to your credit on the books."

"It all sounds very complicated." Peter had lived for so long in an R.A.F. mess where everything had been done for him that he was filled with dismay at the thought of looking after himself.

"You can do the same with the Red Cross food parcels," the commander continued. "Our financial wizard—he's not here to-night, he's out to dinner—has worked out a nominal value for every article that we get in the parcels. Took him weeks to do it. He keeps all the figures in a little book. The mart values fluctuate from day to day, depending on the demand for certain articles. For instance, oatmeal is cheaper in the summer than it is in the winter, and the opposite goes for lemonade powder. Klim is about the most valuable single item."

"Klim?" He felt bewildered by it all.

"Powdered milk," Jonah said. "It comes in the Canadian Red Cross parcels. Wizard stuff—far better than that condensed stuff you get in the English parcels. It keeps better for one thing, and it's easier to use for cooking."

"Chaps do all sorts of things with it," the commander said. "Makes a jolly tenacious paste for mending books or sticking photos up. Chap mended a pipe with it once."

"You can boil water in the tins," Simpson said. He passed over a fire-blackened tin about six inches high and six inches in diameter, to which a wire handle had been fitted.

"A full tin of Klim is worth a hundred and fifty cigarettes on the mart," the commander continued. "When our parcel arrives Tollitt rushes down to the mart with it and—to explain it simply—sells everything which is above par, and buys things that are below par. It means that sometimes our diet is not very varied, but we get more to eat that way."

"It seems very complicated to me," Peter said.

"Ha!" the commander said, "it's the capitalist system." He leaned back against the upright of one of the bunks and twisted a forefinger into his beard. "Y'see, we're all old kriegies, and we've collected a spot of reserve in the food line and can afford to play on the market with it."

"Do you play bridge?" Simpson asked.

"No, I'm afraid I don't," Peter said.

"Don't you learn," Crawford told him. "It becomes a vice in a place like this. Chaps play all day long."

"It's a good way to pass the time, I should think," Peter said.

"You'll find the time will pass quickly enough," the commander told him. "It'll drag a bit at first, but suddenly, one day, you'll stop and realise that you simply haven't time to do all you intend to do. It's simply amazing how little things will fill your life. That's part of the danger—you fritter time away."

"What about escape?" Peter asked.

There was a pause in which he wished he had not spoken. Was it that they were against escape, or had he broken one of the unspoken rules of captivity by speaking of it?

The silence was broken by Tyson who smiled wryly as he spoke. "Come and see us if you have any ideas. But take your time—have a good look round before you make any suggestions. If you get any ideas come and tell us first."

The sudden extinction of all the lights in the room saved Peter from further embarrassment.

"Blast!" the commander spoke out of the darkness. "Where's that lamp of yours, Jack?"

By the light of the small cigarette-lighter flame Peter saw Simpson cross to a cupboard and take down a lamp which he lit with a spill of paper. The lamp was made from old tins fastened one above the other and had one side cut away like an old-fashioned "dark lantern." It gave off a steady golden light, brighter than the smoky red glow in the other messes.

"That's a good lamp," Peter said.

"It's the fuel," Simpson told him. "It's margarine that's been rendered down to extract the water. Expensive, but it gives a clean light. Some of these chaps burn crude margarine, cooking fat or even boot polish—what can they expect?"

"What d'you use as a wick?"

"This one's made of pyjama cord, seems to be more absorbent than anything else. You can use bits of flannel, but I prefer pyjama cord."

Peter looked round at the other messes. The long room, plunged so suddenly into darkness, slowly assumed a new personality as one after another the flickering lamps threw their long shadows across the walls and roof. Conversation had fallen to a murmur, the prisoners closing in to make small groups huddled round the lamps. "What's wrong with the lights?" he asked.

"It's the goons," the commander said. "The S.B.O. had a row with them about the sanitation, so they're carrying out reprisals."

Peter must have shown his bewilderment.

"S.B.O.—Senior British Officer. Goons—Germans," Simpson told him. "Kriegies—p.o.w.'s. You get used to it in time, it's another language."

"You'll forget you've ever been anything else but a

kriegie in a week or two," Crawford said. "That's the danger."

When the lights came on again there were ironic cheers, the lamps were put out and the groups dispersed. Conversation swelled again, and the room was restored to its normal level of noisy shouts and long range conversation.

"What's the latest news from the Middle East?" the commander asked.

Once again Peter felt his inadequacy. He knew nothing about the Middle East. Flying had been enough for him—flying and forgetting about flying when he was not on duty. "I'm not very well up in the Middle East," he said. "There's an army chap in our mess though—he was captured there. He'll know more about it than I do." He couldn't know less, he thought.

Conversation languished. He did not like to ask them any more questions and by now they apparently thought it useless to ask him any. They began to talk among themselves about the international rugger matches. It was not until they had been talking for some time that he realised it was the camp matches they were discussing and not the real thing. "D'you play rugger here?" he asked.

"Where do you play?" Simpson asked.

"Full back."

"Right—we'll give you a trial as soon as the snow clears. Have you played recently?"

"About a month ago."

"Splendid! We'll fix you up with boots. Got any long pants?"

"Long pants?"

"Pitch is a bit stony. Advisable to wear something over your knees—get gravel-rash, y'know."

"I'm afraid I haven't got any," Peter said. He wondered what he had let himself in for.

"I'll lend you a pair," Simpson said.

Conversation languished again.

"Well, I'll be getting back."

They all stood.

"Thanks very much for the dinner." He wanted to ask them all back, but realised that he only owned a sixth of the mess.

"Don't forget, as soon as the snow clears," Simpson said.

"Come and see us again sometime," the commander said. By the way he spoke, it sounded a long and difficult journey.

Back in his own mess he found that the others had returned from their dinner parties and were sitting round the table drinking cocoa. "You are just in time," Otto said. "We have a cup for you." He poured the cocoa from the tall metal jug.

"It'll make you sleep," Loveday said. "I've just been telling these individuals to get to sleep. They need all the sleep they can get. The most important thing about . . ."

"What sort of party did you have?" John asked.

"I never knew I knew so little," Peter said. "I've made a date for you to go along and tell 'em all about the Middle East."

"That's O.K.," John said. "We had a lecture on it the day before I was captured. I've got myself into an amateur dramatic society."

"I've got myself into a rugger match—played on concrete," Peter said.

"We were wrong about that adjutant, Pete." John came and sat beside him on the bunk.

"Which adjutant?"

"The permanent staff chap at *Dulag*."

"In what way?"

"The chaps in the other mess were telling me. It's hush-hush, so don't spread it around, but he's working for us. He lets the Germans think he's a dead-beat and ready to work for them, and all the time he's getting information which he sends back to England."

"How does he send it back?"

"God knows, but he does. But what a rotten sort of job to have."

"You certainly need guts for a job like that," Peter said.

"All the new chaps have got to parade for a short-arm inspection in the morning," Saunders said. He was standing half-undressed, by the side of his bunk.

"What on earth for?" Hugo, already in bed, looked down at him in astonishment.

"Chaps in the other mess told me."

"They pull the leg, I think," Otto said.

The lights flickered on and off twice.

"Five minutes," Loveday said. "In five minutes the lights go out, for the night."

Peter lay in the darkness trying to sleep. The sack of wood shavings was lumpy under his back. He was so near the roof that, if he raised an arm, he could touch its wooden beams. The air up here was acrid with tobacco smoke and thick with the sour smell of overcrowded living. He thought of the men in the mess he had just left; of how they had forced themselves to live in harmony, to make their unpleasant surroundings as bearable as possible. Perhaps we shall be able to do the same, he thought—smooth down the sharp edges, practise a little self-discipline. But that in a way was defeat. Far better to get out of the place, back to the danger and the freedom of the war. He would talk to John about it in the morning. There must be a way of getting out. The group captain had told them that a tunnel was being dug. How many men would they need for that? Perhaps there would be room for one or two more. Yes, he would find out all about it in the morning . . .

From time to time there was a crash and clatter as someone leaped in wooden clogs from an upper bunk, the scuff-

scuffle of the clogs on concrete as the leaper hurried to the latrine, the creak of the opening door and the sudden stench.

All around him he could hear the snores and the heavy breathing of his ninety-odd fellow prisoners. At times a prisoner would shout or mutter in his sleep, sometimes scream in terror—a scream that would be cut short as his neighbour jerked him into waking. At intervals round the room sudden-glowing cigarettes told their story of sleeplessness and boredom.

He thought about the adjutant at *Dulag-Luft*—still carrying out his duty, but in the most unpleasant way. Bearing the scorn and contempt of his fellow-prisoners but all the time doing a hundred times more than they were doing to win the war. He thought of all the traitors of this war, who might, in reality, be spies. How unreasonable to judge, how impossible to give an opinion without being certain of all the facts. He offered a silent apology to that brave man, doing his lonely duty, despised by everyone, even by the Germans he was fooling.

Below in the darkness he heard John sigh and turn restlessly on his bunk. "Are you awake, John?" he whispered.

"I'm just wondering how long I can stick it before I have to go to the lats," John said.

"It's shock." Loveday's voice came didactically from the opposite bunk. "It gets 'em all that way. You'll get over it in time."

Part Two

★

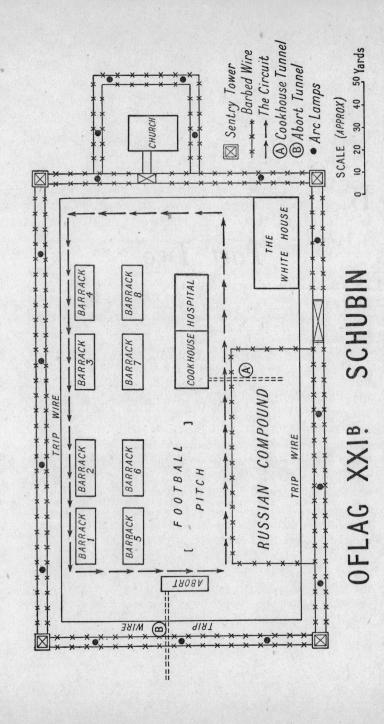

SCALE (APPROX)

0   10   20   30   40   50 Yards

☒ Sentry Tower
—×—×— Barbed Wire
———→ The Circuit
Ⓐ Cookhouse Tunnel
Ⓑ Abort Tunnel
● Arc Lamps

OFLAG XXIB. SCHUBIN

CHURCH

BARRACK 4
BARRACK 3
BARRACK 2
BARRACK 1
BARRACK 8
BARRACK 7
BARRACK 6
BARRACK 5

COOKHOUSE
HOSPITAL

THE WHITE HOUSE

RUSSIAN COMPOUND

FOOTBALL PITCH

TRIP WIRE

TRIP WIRE

TRIP WIRE

ABORT

CHAPTER I

BEFORE THE war *Oflag XXIB* had been a boys' reformatory. When the Germans marched into Poland it was used as a concentration camp, and after the fall of France its barbed-wire defences were strengthened to hold French prisoners of war.

The camp was built on sloping ground and was enclosed by the usual double barbed-wire fence some twelve feet high, guarded at intervals by watch towers armed with machine-guns and fitted with searchlights. The two fences were six feet apart and the space between them, up to a height of about four feet, was filled with coiled barbed-wire.

Some time before Peter's capture, when the French military prisoners had been released to work in German industry, *Oflag XXIB* became a prison camp for British aircrew. Then there had been a number of escapes. The French had been kept in by the threat of reprisals on their families, but the British were not handicapped in this way. They were prisoners of long standing, and they knew the ropes. Before they had been there many weeks a good number of them had already been outside the wire. They did not stay out for long and by the time the Kommandant had sent for the help of the ferrets from their previous camp the punishment cells were already full.

The ferrets completely rewired the compound. They set a new trip-wire thirty feet inside the main fence, and told the prisoners that they would be shot at if they stepped across it. They built more sentry boxes raised on stilts above the wire, and buried seismographs in the earth under the wire. The seismographs were connected to a central

133

control room where any vibration below the earth's surface, caused by tunnelling, was recorded with an ink pen on a revolving paper cyclinder. The prisoners were locked in their barracks from dusk until dawn and during the hours of darkness savage dogs roamed the compound, sniffing at the doors of the barracks, discouraging the prisoners from venturing outside.

To the right of the compound gates at the bottom of the slope, the White House turned its blank and forbidding face towards the road that led to the railway station. Next to it and along the wire which lined the road was a narrow compound reserved for Russian prisoners who worked on the surrounding farms. This compound, inside the main camp, formed yet another barrier between the British prisoners and the world outside.

Behind the White House on slightly higher ground, was another building, once the home of the school staff, now used as the camp hospital and cookhouse. A small church stood in a compound of its own, an angular red-brick church in which a number of prisoners worshipped every Sunday. On the left of the hospital and separated from the road by the Russian compound were the stony football pitch and the latrine, known even to the English by its German name—*abort*. Inside the *abort* were two long deep trenches covered by rough wooden seats for forty-eight people. In the mornings the *abort* was always crowded and a long queue stretched half-way round the football pitch, almost to the hospital.

The rest of the compound was on steeply sloping ground, and terraced into this slope were the squat and ugly single-story brick barracks in which the prisoners lived a hundred to a room.

The gates of the compound were open now and a thin line of guards, their heads bent to the rain, rifles slung across their backs, filed in past the White House and struggled their way up the mud-covered slope towards the barrack

blocks. It was early morning, and the rain fell inexhaustibly
from a solid sky, hammering on the roofs of the sentry
boxes, relentlessly pounding the sodden ground into a sea
of sticky mud. Rain dripped from the barbed-wire and ran
gurgling into the deep ditch which had been dug outside
the wire to discourage tunnelling.

Inside Barrack No 4 the air was damp from the water
that seeped up through the rotten concrete floor, from the
moisture that oozed from the walls, from the rows of
washing, from the breath of a hundred prisoners.

Peter woke slowly and thrust his head from under the
thin German blanket. He was fully dressed, even to his
issue R.A.F. greatcoat. He wore a woollen skull-cap on his
head and mittens on his hands. The coal issue had been
stopped again and they had gone to bed early, huddled
fully dressed beneath their blankets. A film of water lay on
the grey blanket over his head, and the woodwork of the
bunk on which he lay was damp.

It was his turn to be stooge. Loveday and Otto had
insisted on taking over the duty for the first few weeks in
order to give the newcomers time to settle in. They had
settled in all right. The last two months seemed more like
two years.

He lay for a moment under the blankets, mustering the
will-power to get out of bed. A bugle call from the German
Kommandantur had been his alarm clock, and in a few
minutes the guards would be here to unlock the doors and
let him out. It was one of his duties to go to the cookhouse
for hot water for the morning tea. There would be a
concentrated rush of twelve stooges from eight barrack
blocks; ninety-six men, all trying to get there first. Those
at the end of the queue would find that the water had gone
off the boil, and it would be nearly time for roll-call before
they could get back to the mess, to face seven pairs of
disapproving eyes.

He crawled from under his blankets, and was pulling on

the wooden clogs which lay beside his pillow when the door crashed open and two guards, clumsy in their jackboots and camouflaged mackintosh capes, stood wetly in the doorway. "'*Raus*, '*raus!*" they shouted.

The prisoners who were awake replied as one man. They breathed into their reply all their hatred of the German guards, all their contempt for the Third Reich. "—— off!" they shouted, and buried themselves once more under their shoddy blankets. It was a fruitless gesture, they knew they had to get up; but it was a gesture. It was their morning litany.

As soon as the guards had gone Peter grabbed the tall metal jug from the table, threw in a handful of tea leaves and squelched in his clogs across the muddy compound towards the cookhouse. From all directions weird figures at various stages of undress were converging on this spot. The first dozen men in the queue would stand under the shelter of an overhanging corrugated iron porch. The rest would stand in the rain.

Peter found himself behind Bandy Beecham, who was wearing rugger shorts. Bandy's theory was that it was easier to dry your legs than it was to dry your trousers. He seemed unaffected by the cold.

"Coming over to the theatre to-day, Howard? We've still got two more sets to paint—the show has to be ready by Monday week." He looked at Peter accusingly over the turned-up collar of his cut-down issue greatcoat. Most of them had hacked their coats down to fingertip length, using the spare material to make slippers, costumes for the theatre or civilian clothes for the Escape Committee. Bandy's coat finished in a ragged fringe below which his red and naked legs curved aggressively into enormous wooden clogs.

"I'll come if I can, but I'm pretty busy at the moment. Perhaps I'll be able to look in for an hour this afternoon." Peter had been recruited by Bandy to help paint the scenery for the coming camp concert. As the commander had predicted, his life was now so filled with necessary chores that he found it difficult to fit them all in. "How did the rehearsal go?" He wanted to show some interest, to atone for his failure to turn up the previous day.

"Complete chaos." Bandy assumed his role of the harassed impresario. "First we couldn't get started because they were using the theatre as a damned lecture hall, then the fairy queen had to go off to play rugger. If this goes on much longer I shall chuck the whole thing up. No one appreciates it anyway."

"You wait till you hear the applause on opening night," Peter said. "You'll think it's worth it then."

"If there ever is an opening night." Bandy retired into gloomy silence.

When Peter arrived back in the mess, he found that John had buttered two thin slices of black bread for each man and was spreading them thinly with jam. He remembered how, in the early days of their captivity, they had left the jam-pot on the table for each man to help himself. He remembered how unsatisfactory this had been; how an unjust estimation of the amount taken by one's neighbour had led to a rapid spiral upwards in the jam consumption of the mess.

He put the jug down and stirred in several spoonfuls of condensed milk. The milk, too, had once been left freely on the table. He remembered the row when Otto had discovered Hugo helping himself to a spoonful after the others had gone out to roll-call. Now everything was shared out by the stooges. It seemed fairer that way. He wondered if they would ever attain the equanimity of the older kriegies; it didn't look much like it.

"Come on, show a leg! Brew up!" he chanted.

In each of the other eleven messes the morning's stooge was rousing his charges in his own way. There was a general stirring throughout the block; groans, grunts, yawns and sleepy badinage. The men in the next mess continued the bridge post-mortem which had been suppressed by the angry shouts of their tired neighbours the night before.

In Peter's mess there was a feeling of strain. Loveday had been riding them ever since they had arrived. At first his advice, although given in a didactic, difficult manner, had been welcome; but they had outgrown any need of Loveday's nursing. They wanted to be left alone.

John sat reading while he ate his bread and jam. It seemed to Peter that he used his book as a defence against Loveday's conversation.

"You individuals read too much," Loveday said. "Reading maketh a fool, man."

"What did you say?" Hugo paused in astonishment, half-way between his bed and the table; he was still continually astonished at the things the others said.

"I said, reading maketh a fool, man."

"It isn't fool," Hugo said. "It's full—F-U-L-L. Reading maketh a *full* man."

"Well, that's more than you can say for this breakfast." It was Saunders' attempt to stop the argument before it was under way. He might just as well have tried to stop the rain.

"It's fool," Loveday said. "Thomas Babington Macaulay."

"Bacon," John said it through a mouthful of bread and jam, without looking up from his book.

"Kindly do not address me with your mouth full, Clinton. We have all the time in the world here. There is no hurry at all. Now, what did you say?"

"I said Bacon—Francis Bacon."

Loveday drew himself up to his full height, his face deep red. "Macaulay!"

"*Bacon!*" Hugo shouted. John had retired from the argument, back into his book, as he always retired when the argument grew noisy.

"Christ!" The voice came from the next mess. "Are you chaps still arguing about food?"

"Everybody reads too much." Loveday ignored the interruption and considered the argument about the authority won. "There's too much wireless, too much cinema. Nobody has time to think. Why don't you chaps do what I do—sit down for a couple of hours every day and just think!"

"Why don't you do it at mealtimes?" Hugo snapped.

Loveday was well under way now. "Because it's not my time for meditation, that's why. I can't think while I'm eating. That's why I don't read with my meals."

"You don't half talk, though," Saunders said.

"I talk at mealtimes because it promotes digestion. And I meditate in the afternoon because then the body's metabolism is at its lowest ebb. I read just before lunch and in the early evening because at those times the human mind is in its most receptive condition."

"You do read, then?" Hugo seemed unable to let it rest.

"I read to learn—not to escape from life. Reading for me is a communion of two minds. I only read one book——"

"*A Textbook of Psychology*," Saunders said.

"Exactly. And let me tell you that a careful study of this great work——"

"On *appel!*" It was Stewart, the block commander. "Come on, all outside." He stopped at the doorway of the mess. "Your turn to stooge to-day, chaps."

"Right," Peter said. "When do you want us?"

"Three o'clock in the *abort*."

"O.K."

"All this stooging nonsense," Loveday said. "They'll never get out. Wasting everyone else's time as well as their own. Why don't they——"

"Officer at the gate!" It was Otto, watching from the window of their mess, the only window that looked out on to the path leading up from the main gate.

"All outside," Stewart shouted. "Officer coming up the hill. All outside!"

"I'm not going on *appel*," Hugo said. "I'm *krank* this morning."

"O.K.," Stewart said. "Get back into bed."

"Come on, John." Peter snatched his greatcoat from the bunk and hurled it round his shoulders. John picked up his book, finished his mug of tea and collected his coat from the lower bunk.

"Good chap, Marcus Aurelius. Listen to this." He read from the book. "*They seek for themselves private retiring places, as country villages, the seashore, mountains; yea thou thyself art wont to long much after such places. But all this thou must know proceeds from simplicity in the highest degree. At what time soever thou wilt, it is in thy power to retire into thyself, and to be at rest, and free from all businesses.*"

"Free from all businesses, indeed," Peter said. "He didn't have to live in a prison camp."

Outside it was still raining, and a few of the prisoners stood miserably in small groups in front of each barrack block, watched by their no less miserable guards. The *Lageroffizier* was just coming into the compound, through the gate at the bottom of the slope. Stiffly returning the salute of the guard, he picked his way carefully up the muddy path.

Half-way up the slope, he looked towards the barrack blocks, and began to walk more slowly. It was a point of honour, a battle of wills. The officer refused to arrive before all the prisoners were ready on parade, the prisoners refused to wait on parade for the officer to arrive.

In the past there had been trouble on this score, and the morning *appel* had sometimes lasted long into the afternoon. This had been a punishment for all; for the prisoners, for the guards and for the officer himself. More for the Germans than for their prisoners, because the prisoners had little else to do with their time. It was, in a way, a victory for them. Eventually they had become bored with standing around, and came to a tacit understanding with their guards. It was understood that they would parade in their own time, but would be ready when the officer reached the top of the hill. But he never trusted them. Seeing the ranks still incomplete by the time he was half-way up the hill, he always became frightened and walked more slowly. He would lose face if he reached the top of the hill before the prisoners were ready. But he had to keep on walking; he would lose face also if he stopped. The stooges, watching him from the windows, left it until the last minute before shouting "Officer coming up the hill." There was then a sudden and astonishing exodus through doors and windows by half-dressed, seemingly panic-stricken kriegies. The officer resumed his normal pace and honour was satisfied.

He was met at the top of the slope by the British adjutant, a short man who always manœuvred to obtain the advantage of the higher ground, so that he could look down on the sallow bespectacled German as he returned his morning salute.

The prisoners stood in fives and slowly the guards walked up and down the ranks, counting them. It was said that the guards could only count in fives. Another guard went through the barrack block to count the *krank im Zimmer*. The officer stood watching, the rain dripping from the shiny black peak of his service cap and soaking into the olive-green of his cape. The prisoners waited like a herd of passive cattle, wet now, but knowing that the rain would stop sometime.

The guard who had counted the sick in bed reported to the *Obergefreiter*, who in turn reported to the *Feldwebel*, who reported to the *Lageroffizier*. The *Lageroffizier* saluted the British adjutant, and the prisoners were dismissed. They would not be bothered again by the Germans until the afternoon *appel*.

Back in the barrack block, John took the breakfast things to rinse them under the cold water tap in the washhouse, while Peter stayed behind to sweep the floor and scrub the wooden table. Otto and Loveday lay full length on their bunks. Hugo sat on the edge of his, studying his hair in a small hand mirror.

Peter attacked the rough damp concrete floor with a broom he had borrowed from the next-door mess. It was bad enough to sweep up after people when they were not there, but when it was raining and they lay all over the place so that he had to sweep round them, it was worse. He lifted Hugo's feet from the floor and swung them on to the bed.

"Here, steady on!" Hugo said.

"How the hell d'you expect me to sweep under the bunks?" Peter asked.

"Shouldn't bother, I never do." Hugo returned to his study.

On the other side of the table Loveday, in the lower bunk, was explaining to Otto, in the upper, exactly why it was that Poland lay so far behind England in the forward march of civilisation. Otto listened politely. He had spent some months in a *Gestapo* gaol where, it was rumoured, torture had been used to extract information. He never spoke of it, but for Peter he still retained that aura of mystery which cloaked all those to whom violence had been done. He would have liked to talk to Otto intimately, to hear his story, but Otto never encouraged intimacy. He lived quietly within the secret reclusion of his past experience, giving himself only to Alan Loveday, whom he treated with a tenderness that the others could not understand.

Saunders usually spent the morning walking round the circuit or watching a football match. He was not a reading man. Wet mornings were a trial to him, and now he came and stood awkwardly by the table. "Pete, d'you mind if I light a *Stufa*?"

"For God's sake!" Peter was angry at first, but saw the look in Saunders' eyes. "Oh, all right—but mind you clear the mess up after you. You'd better open the window, too."

Saunders took the *Stufa* from under his bunk. It looked like a rusty battered coffee percolator. The top section held water, the middle was fitted with a patent draught-forcing arrangement of his own invention, and the bottom, made from a Klim tin, was the firebox. The *Stufa* burned small shavings of wood that Saunders had cut from a plank with one of the table knives.

Soon the mess was full of smoke which quickly spread to the adjoining rooms.

"PUT THAT BLOODY THING OUT!" The shouted protests came from the nearby messes.

"Nearly boiling." It was Saunders' boast that he could boil half a cupful of water before anyone else knew that the *Stufa* was alight. "O.K., chaps, it's out now." Shaking with suppressed laughter, he put the *Stufa* back under the bunk, closed the window and sat down at the table, preparing to shave.

"SHUT THE BLOODY WINDOW!" someone shouted from the next mess.

"It's all right, it's all right," Saunders said. "I've shut it."

"You're not shaving here, are you, Saunders?" It was Hugo speaking from his bunk.

"Why not?"

"The washhouse is the place for shaving."

"I can't shave there, it's fully occupied."

"What d'you mean?"

"I mean it's fully occupied. If you'd had the energy to go and wash this morning you could have seen it yourself. You're no more sick than I am."

"I'm sick of you turning this mess into a gentlemen's lavatory." Hugo put the mirror back on the shelf above his head. "Also, it may surprise you to hear that I had a cold shower and a shave before any of you were awake this morning. I just didn't feel like going on *appel*, that's all."

"Lucky we don't all feel like that," Saunders said.

When John came back with the breakfast things, Peter had finished the floor and was scrubbing the table with a nail brush.

"There's a hell of a mess in the washhouse." John seemed amused. "Go and have a look."

"I'm too busy," Peter said.

"Go on—have a look. I'll finish the table."

"Ah, well, if you insist. I'll get some more water while I'm there." He took the metal jug from the shelf and made his way down the long room, through a small lobby just large enough to house the brick cooking stove, and into the washhouse which they shared with the next-door barrack.

It was a simple brick-built room with whitewashed walls and a concrete floor. There were long cement troughs with rows of dripping taps, and wooden benches on which some prisoners were washing their clothes. Beneath a rough shower made fom a length of rubber hose and a punctured tin, a naked figure danced under ice-cold water, while his laundering neighbours, cursing, clutched their washing and retreated from the broadcast splashes.

The place was even more crowded than usual this morning, and more noisy. Above the tumult of shouting, singing and slapping of wet clothes on the wooden benches, Peter heard a cautious tap-tap-tap. In one corner of the room a man was breaking through the concrete floor with a chisel made from a window-fastener.

Tyson and the bearded commander were washing their shirts on one of the benches near the door.

"What's all this in aid of?" Peter asked.

"The crazy gang from the next block." The commander's beard bristled with indignation. "How can a man do his dhobying in a row like this?"

"They haven't a chance," Tyson said. "Just making a bloody nuisance of themselves."

"It won't be for long, that's one thing. They'll have the goons round here like flies round honey." The commander slapped his washing with a hand the size of a spade. "A damn' fool effort like that won't last for long."

When Peter arrived back in the mess Saunders was carefully sorting out his "rubbish," the mysterious blanket-covered bundle he had brought from *Dulag-Luft*. At first the rest of them had been enthusiastic about the cooking utensils—saucepans made from old cans, and baking dishes from rolled-out jam tins—that it had contained. They had not been so enthusiastic about the mass of raw material which he had brought along. There were short lengths of wire, pieces of string, tins of rusty nails, nuts and bolts, a penknife with a broken blade, bunches of flattened-out tins, photographs torn from magazines—all the hundred and one things once jealously hoarded by the schoolboy, now valuable again in the eyes of the prisoner of war.

Hugo, impelled by moral indignation, had gone for a walk. John was reading through the argument between Otto and Loveday, which had now progressed to religion and psychology—the ultimate goal of all Loveday's arguments.

"What's going on out there?" Saunders asked, looking up from his litter-covered blanket.

"Some chaps from the next block starting a tunnel," Peter told him.

"Then we shan't have any peace until it's discovered," Loveday said.

"Can't say we have much now," Saunders muttered, "chaps nagging at you all the time."

"It's stopped raining, Pete," John said. "Let's go for a walk."

"I haven't time, I've got to get the lunch ready."

"'Morning, chaps!" A stranger stood at the doorway of

the mess. "D'you mind if I stooge from your window? We've got a *dienst* on in the washhouse."

"There you are," Loveday said. "What did I tell you?"

"O.K., John," Peter said. "Let's go for a walk."

Out in the compound, the prisoners were taking exercise. Round and round, just inside the wire, pacing the eternal treadmill of the path they had worn with their restless feet; parallel to that other, fainter pathway a few yards outside the wire, worn by the feet of their guards.

On the circuit, as it was called, the prisoners walked according to their mood; some in groups of three or four, talking loudly or chaffing one another; others in twos, deep in discussion or reminiscence—perhaps planning an escape. Some walked alone, hands in pockets, heads sunk on chests, blindly miserable, locked in a prison within a prison, desperate in their loneliness. These walked with their eyes fixed on the ground before their feet. There was no point in lifting their eyes. If they lifted them they could only see the wire, and the wire reminded them of their captivity. So they mooched slowly round with their hands in their pockets, and their eyes unfocused on the ground; ignoring the existence of the wire.

And the man who to-day walked slowly in his loneliness would to-morrow pace it out with the crowd. It was a terrible periodic misery that gripped them all at times, and then lifted miraculously so that they walked with their eyes raised and saw the sky again. It was difficult, when gripped by the misery, to remember that this would pass.

"Thank God it's stopped raining," Peter said. He looked at the camp, sodden underfoot but washed clean by the rain. "Life's impossible when everyone's inside."

"It's pretty impossible anyway," John said. "It's time we got cracking and got out of it."

"You can say that again," Peter said, "and go on saying it. Every idea we've had has been squashed by the Committee. We were taken prisoner about three years too late, that's our trouble. Every possible place has been used at least once already. Look at that job they've just started in the wash-house. They only started it there because there was nowhere else. Even Tyson says they haven't a hope."

"He amuses me," John said. "He's always so furtive. He's the typical cloak-and-dagger merchant—I'm sure he talks to himself in code."

"He knows all there is to know about tunnelling," Peter said. "He's got it all buttoned up."

"He may have, but he's still here."

"He's been out several times. Once you're outside the wire, it must be a matter of luck how far you get—absolute luck. It's getting out that takes the ingenuity."

"I suppose a tunnel is the only way?"

For Peter, the next best thing to escaping was talking about escape. He began to ride his hobbyhorse. "Examine the problem," he said. "What is it? To get outside the wire. Right. There are three ways—over the wire, under the wire, or through the wire. You've only got three choices."

"The first one's out as far as I'm concerned," John said.

"I agree. You'd never get away with it—and even if you *did* get over you couldn't take any kit with you. You wouldn't get very far."

"There are two ways of going through: By the gate or cutting through the wire itself." John was riding with him now, knee to knee.

"Cutting through the wire is pretty impossible," Peter said. "That leaves the gate. And there are two ways of doing that."

"A bluff or a stowaway."

"Exactly. To stow away there's the bread cart or the rubbish cart. Bluffing is no good unless you look like one of the goons, and neither of us do." He looked at John with his fringe of downy beard and grinned.

"The carts have just about had it," John said. "They've been tried so often that the goons examine every inch of them. There's the night-cart, too—you'd forgotten that."

Peter shuddered.

"A chap did it once," John said. "Bribed the Pole who was driving it only to half-fill the tank and sat up to his neck in the stuff. Stark naked, with his clothes tied up in a groundsheet on top of his head."

"Wonder he didn't die before he got outside," Peter said. "Did he get away with it?"

"He was caught at the gate. Now they make the Poles fill the carts right up to the top."

"It'll have to be a tunnel," Peter said. "It's the only way." It was the conclusion they had reached so often before.

"It certainly seems like it," John said. "But where? The only place we haven't thought of is the church." He suddenly became excited. "Why not? It's quite near the wire and I don't believe the goons ever go in there."

"How should we get in? There's a wire fence round it, y'know." This was no longer wishful talking; this was a possibility.

"Go in with the morning service, stay there all day digging, and come out with the chaps from evening service. A Frenchman called Atger did it in the last war, I remember my father telling me about it. We could take enough food in with us to last all day, and work in comfort. We could make the trap right underneath the altar."

"How should we dispose of the clay?"

"Oh, I expect we could tuck it away under the floor, or in the roof. Or failing that we could distribute it among the people at evening service and get them each to bring a bit out."

"I wonder what the padre would say." He felt that there must be a snag in it somewhere.

"He needn't know."

"It's well worth trying," Peter said. "Let's go and have a word with Tyson."

"Better keep this one to ourselves," John said.

"Tyson's all right," Peter told him. "I promised I'd tell him if we had an idea. It'd be silly to go into it alone, it's too good a scheme to mess up by not preparing properly. Besides, he's on the Escape Committee."

"I'd rather try it on our own."

"We can't do that. Someone might be working there already without our knowing it. There probably is." He suddenly became despondent. "There's bound to be a snag of some sort. It's too good a place not to have been tried before."

"Come on," John said. "We'll go and see him, we can't do any harm."

They found Tyson sucking an empty pipe and putting the finishing touches to a civilian jacket he was making out of a blanket.

"'Morning," Peter said. "May we come in?" It was the mess in which he had dined on the night of his arrival.

"Come in, come in!" Tyson cleared a stool and moved from his own seat to the bed. "Come in and sit down." He looked at them inquiringly.

"We've got a scheme for a tunnel," Peter said.

Tyson grinned. "What, another?"

Briefly they outlined the plan. It sounded good to them. While they were talking Tyson filled his pipe and lit it from the stub of John's cigarette.

"Yes, it's a good idea," he said. "I've had it suggested before. Unfortunately the chapel is on parole and must not be used for escape purposes. That also applies to anything to do with the theatre. I'm afraid you'll have to think again."

Peter looked at Tyson quietly smoking and sewing at his jacket and felt the hopelessness of it all. Here was a man who had been here for years, and had tried to escape ever since he had been here. And they were only on the fringe; had not even started. At first he had thought it would be easy. "Get to a permanent camp and then make your plan." He looked round him at the now well-known squalor of the large room and felt the misery rise inside him like a sudden wave of nausea. He fought it down again, tried to drive it back, refuse to acknowledge it.

"Is there any chance of getting into a scheme that's already started?" he asked.

"There are only two tunnels going at the moment," Tyson said. "The one from the *abort* and that crazy idea from next door. The *abort* one's full up and I wouldn't advise the other." He hesitated for a moment, then, having considered, spoke with more enthusiasm. "As a matter of fact, I'm thinking of opening up an old tunnel that's been lying derelict for some time. We had to abandon it because of flooding. It's worth having another shot at, anyway."

"D'you want any help?" Peter asked.

Tyson puffed at his pipe. "We haven't decided to open it up yet. I'm going down this afternoon to have a look at it."

"Where's it from?" John asked.

"It's from the cookhouse behind the hospital—where you get the hot water in the morning. If we do open it up again we shall need some enthusiastic types and I'll keep you two in mind. You won't get into the digging team right away but I might be able to start you off in one of the dispersal squads."

"Thanks very much." Peter rose to his feet. "It's a pity about the church."

"We must stand by our word," Tyson said, "even if the goons don't."

Out on the circuit again John was enthusiastic. "Well, we've got somewhere," he said. "It was worth having the idea just for that."

But Peter did not want to be enthusiastic. They had been enthusiastic too often during the last few weeks. He wanted to wait now until it was certain. To talk about it now would spoil it. But he felt the excitement inside him, making him walk faster, walk as thought he were really going somewhere instead of marching like a processional caterpillar round the circuit of the wire.

They walked quickly without talking, overtaking others, slipping on the damp clay as the path dipped down towards the football pitch. They passed the *abort*, skirted the Russian compound, passed the White House, the hospital and the cookhouse—significant now because of its abandoned tunnel. They climbed the far slope, came round behind the barracks and down past the *abort* again.

"Did you know that Otto was in the *abort* scheme?" John said.

"No, is he?"

"Nor did I until the other day. I found a heap of old clothes covered in damp clay under his bed. I was looking for a potato I'd dropped. When I taxed him he told me all about it. D'you know, the thing's about fifteen feet deep. I think they stand a pretty good chance of getting away with it."

"How far have they got?"

"They've done about ninety feet already. They'll be out in about a month—that is if the goons don't decide to dig another *abort* and fill in the old one."

"It's certainly time they did," Peter said. He could still smell it from where they were, on the far side of the football pitch. "Where does the tunnel actually start?"

"From the side of the trench. You have to get right down into it to get into the tunnel. Not a job for the squeamish. They struck water about half-way, and they have to crawl through inches of it. Those clothes of Otto's stank to high heaven—he usually keeps them down the tunnel, but they had to get out in a hurry the other day and they hadn't time to change."

"How did they manage to get from the *abort* up to the barrack block in their tunnelling clothes without being spotted by the goons?"

"I didn't ask him. I suppose they put greatcoats on or something. They couldn't have chosen a more unpleasant place to start a tunnel from, really . . . Although a kriegie never gets a chance to get far from an *abort*. I tried to escape from the window of one coming up through Italy, and I've been hounded by them ever since."

"Did you do that, too?" Peter was amused. It was extraordinary how like Roy John was, with his dark vitality hidden beneath a cloak of indolence.

"What?"

"Try to climb out of the lavatory window."

"If anyone wants to escape he's almost forced to go to the *abort* to do it," John said. "If he wants to eat or change his clothes while he's escaping, he has to do it in the *abort*." He laughed. "I used to eat my tuck in the lavatory at prep school. It was the only place one could be alone."

"It's the only place you can be alone here," Peter said. "You *can* be alone there—but at what a cost!"

"Not in the big one you can't," John said, "not in the forty-eight seater!"

CHAPTER II

WHEN THEY had eaten their lunch, Peter and John began to prepare the evening meal by peeling the twelve half-rotten potatoes which were the ration for the day. The potatoes were bruised and black, but to make them clean more than half would have had to be cut away. They compromised, cutting away only the parts that were already putrid. They put the potatoes in water in the square baking-dish which Saunders had made from rolled-out Klim tins, and Peter took them out to find a place on the cooking stove.

There was not much room on the stove but he managed to get the tin near the edge, where it was almost cold. At intervals he went out to push the tin a little nearer the centre; but as eleven other cooks were each doing the same thing, the tins merely followed one another in endless procession round the top of the stove.

"D'you think anything will come of Tyson's idea?" John lay on his mattress, gazing at the bottom of Peter's bunk a few inches above his head.

"Shouldn't bank on it." Peter was busy on a rough design that he was making for the theatre scenery. He drew on a piece of cardboard cut from a Red Cross food box. "Anyway, if anything does come of it we shall only be on the fringe. I should have been much happier if the church idea had come off."

"The church and the theatre would have to be on parole. I wonder about the hospital?"

"Bound to be," Peter said. "You couldn't do it. If the goons closed that down we'd be in a hell of a state."

"It's a stupid thing, giving parole." John kicked the foot of his bunk and sent a shower of shavings flying from the upper mattress. "The church would have been an ideal place."

"If there were no parole there'd be no church, theatre or hospital. It's the only way we can get the costumes and paint for the scenery. We've got to strike a balance. After all, we'd both be pretty lost without the theatre."

"I wouldn't mind doing without it for a chance to escape."

"The two things don't necessarily follow." Peter forced himself to concentrate on the drawing.

By two-thirty the potatoes were half-boiled and he took them off the fire and brought them back into the mess, where he mashed them with a tin nailed to the end of a piece of wood.

"They still look pretty black," John said.

"The salmon'll hide it," Peter told him.

They opened the two tins of salmon and mixed the fish with the mashed potatoes, adding a little Klim and pepper and salt. The mixture still looked depressingly grey.

"I'll make some gravy," Peter said. "That'll hide it."

"If we put a little more Klim in, it won't look so grey."

"This'll fix it." Peter was mixing brown gravy powder with water. As he stirred he tried to forget Tyson's tunnel, to think of the scenery that he was designing. That, at least, was a fact, not merely a vague possibility.

"I think we could do with some more Klim," John said. "I say, I've just realised why they call it Klim—it's milk spelt backwards!"

A balcony would be the thing, Peter was thinking, with stairs on the prompt side; a good heavy-looking carved oak balustrade.

"Should we put a little more in, d'you think?"

"Yes, shove it in." Would it be possible to make a piano out of plywood? A piano would look well with that coloured shawl thrown over it, and a bowl of artificial flowers. There was a chap in Block 5 who made jolly good artificial flowers. He'd have roses, mixed red and white roses looking as though they had just been cut from the garden.

"I think we can spare it," John said.

Peter came back to earth. "How much have we got?"

"About half a tin."

"Better not. Put some more breadcrumbs in if you like. Here's the gravy." He poured the thick brown liquid over the mixture in the tin. "There, that should camouflage it all right."

John stepped back and examined it. "Looks a bit soggy."

"It'll stiffen up," Peter told him. "They always do."

"A little Klim would help."

"We can't afford it." Peter was firm about this. "Bread'll have the same effect."

John grated in some more breadcrumbs. "What shall we give them as a sweet?"

"Oh, God—of course!" Peter had forgotten the sweet. "Let's have cheese and biscuits."

"There'll be a hell of a row if we don't make a sweet. We gave them cheese and biscuits yesterday."

"Let's have stewed prunes." It was all he could think of.

"Are there any soaked?"

"I thought you soaked some yesterday."

"I thought you were going to."

"Well, I didn't, so we can't have prunes. What do you suggest?"

"We could fry some biscuits."

"They've got to be soaked, too." He would have done almost anything to be relieved of the responsibility of being cook.

"I'll soak 'em," John said. "You look after the pie." He took eight large round biscuits and put them to soak in water in another tin.

With a fork Peter drew a stylised pattern on the smooth

top of the salmon pie. "There—that'll come out all right, I hope. Now I must get down to the theatre."

"What's the time?"

"It's about three o'clock."

"We've got to stooge at three."

"Hell—I'd forgotten all about that. Bandy'll be furious. Where do we have to go?"

"I'm in the White House, you're in the lower *abort*, I think. We'll just make it if we hurry."

In the lower *abort* behind the football pitch, Peter found the tunnellers already assembled.

"Come on!" Stewart said. "Where the hell've you been?"

"Sorry, I've been cooking."

"So've I for that matter. There's your contact, standing on the corner over there. See him?" He pointed to a muffled figure who stood at the far end of the football pitch, apparently watching a group of prisoners throwing a rugby ball about. It was Saunders. "If he blows his nose, give us a shout." Stewart began quickly to strip off his clothes.

Peter watched the figure at the far end of the football pitch and listened to the clipped conversation of the men behind him. They were talking of the air pump and of wood for shoring the tunnel. Presently he heard the clack-wheeze, clack-wheeze of the pump, and knew that they had started work.

He began to grow stiff and cold. He knew that many yards below his feet men were sweating and straining in the slime of the tunnel. He knew that he was helping them, but that was not enough; he wanted to dig. He wanted to be in a scheme himself. If only Tyson decided to open up the tunnel from the cookhouse he would have a chance. At first he would only be stooging as he was now, but he would have a footing. He would know that if the tunnel succeeded he would have a place in it, however low down. And he might eventually get into the digging team. Since his arrival at the camp he had looked on the tunnellers as a special breed of men, much as at school he had looked on those with tassels to their caps.

At intervals seven-pound jam tins full of clay were hauled to the surface. The clay was emptied into the adjacent *aborts*, and pushed under with long poles. The smell was almost overpowering. He pressed his nose close to the draughty window, and concentrated on Saunders, whose muffled figure was becoming difficult to see in the gathering dusk.

Suddenly he saw a flash of white. Saunders was blowing his nose. "Goon approaching," Peter shouted. "Stewart!"

"O.K., watch Saunders." Hurriedly Stewart began to dismantle the air pump. "If he scratches his head it means that the coast is clear again. Give us a shout if he does."

He heard the air pump being hidden and the scuffling as the men who had been working on the surface dispersed to various seats in their role of involuntary visitors.

He saw Saunders scratch his head, and gave them the "All clear!"

He heard the pump begin to work again, and presently the splash of falling clay.

At four-thirty Stewart called a halt. It was time for the tunnellers to come up and wash before their tea.

"Let's have some jam," Saunders pleaded. "I'm frozen through to the marrow."

"The rule is," Peter said, "jam yesterday, jam to-morrow, but never jam to-day." He cracked the old, old joke, hiding his hurt beneath the badinage.

"I know, I know," Saunders said. The joke was wearing a little thin, even for him. "But we've had the mail to-day— let's have a bash."

"If we have jam for tea, we have no jam for breakfast," Peter said. "Please yourselves—we'll have a vote. All those in favour? . . . Fair enough—let to-morrow look after itself."

"Bandy Beecham called in this afternoon to see why you hadn't gone down to help him with the scenery," Hugo said. "I told him you were busy. He wants to know if you'll go over to-morrow."

"Thanks." Peter put a minute quantity of jam on to each slice of bread and butter.

Otto came in and sat down; he looked tired. "Ah, we have jam. That is good."

"Sheer prodigality," Peter told him, and gave him some extra jam.

"I've had a letter from my Aunt Grace," Hugo said. He was cutting his slice of bread into thin fingers, maintaining the convention of afternoon tea. "She's got a Siamese cat. Used to write to me every week while I was on the squadron."

"What—the cat?" Saunders was spreading his jam lovingly into every corner of the slice of bread.

"No, the aunt—about the cat. She's worried about his habits. Used to send me bulletins regularly every week. She's sent telegrams before now. I thought I'd got away from it all when I was shot down, but now she's started writing to me here. I suppose I'll have to use my precious letter-forms to write to the old bitch."

"I shouldn't bother." Saunders took a bite that accounted for a third of his slice of bread.

"Oh, but I must. I have expectations, great expectations." Hugo took a small bite from one of the fingers of bread and jam and replaced the remainder on the table in front of him.

"This also is funny," Otto said. "I have a letter to-day. I do not have many letters; this one is the first I have received in six months. Many months ago I receive a sweater from the Red Cross, and inside the sweater is sewn a piece of paper with the address of the lady who had knitted the sweater. I write to this lady in South Africa, and thank her for the sweater. I have now a letter from her. She says that she is sorry and it is all a mistake, she knitted the sweater for someone on Active Service."

"She ought to try it sometime," Saunders said. "What d'you think—my old woman's joined the W.A.A.F. Says it'll be more companionable. I'll give 'er companionable when I get back . . ."

"Were there any letters for me?" John asked.

"They all looked like bills," Saunders said. "I threw 'em on the fire."

"There was nothing for you." Loveday's meditation was over for the day. "I looked specially," he added darkly. "I've been observing you, Clinton, and I've come to the conclusion that you're the type that can't exist without extraneous stimuli. Letters are very important to you, aren't they?"

"Well—I like getting them."

"There you are. Now, the only way a man can be complete——"

"Young Simpson got caught this afternoon," Saunders said.

"Caught doing what?" John seemed grateful for the interruption.

"Trying to get out in the rubbish cart. He hid under some old tins they were carting away from the cookhouse. They got as far as the gate, and one of the ferrets started poking about in the rubbish with his steel spike. He got young Simmy right up the arse with it, and that was that. Marched 'im straight off to the cooler."

"You'll never learn," Loveday said. "Why run away from life? If only you individuals would realise that this incarceration was sent to try you. Then you would grasp it with both hands, instead of running away from it."

"Why running away from life?" Peter said, fighting down his misery. "Surely it's just as much running away to stay here and accept it."

"If it was your fate to be taken prisoner," Loveday said, "it was your fate. There's no running away from that."

"How d'you know it isn't your fate to escape?" He knew

that it was uselss to argue with Loveday, but now he could not help it.

"You'd be given a sign," Loveday said.

"You treat fate like a fruit machine," Peter said. "Stop it working when it's most convenient. How did you know that it wasn't your fate to go down with the aircraft? Why did you bale out with a parachute?"

"The pilot told me to."

"Supposing he hadn't? Supposing he'd been killed? Would you have baled out then?"

"It was fate that he wasn't killed," Loveday said. "Everything is ordained by fate."

"What absolute cock!" Peter could contain himself no longer. He rose to his feet and blundered out on to the circuit. To escape from the mess and take his misery with him, out on to the now deserted and muddy path. He too, had received a letter that afternoon, a letter from his mother, written on an official letter-form, telling him that Roy had been shot down over France. "I pray that he has been taken prisoner," his mother had said, "and that one day he will join you in the camp . . ."

CHAPTER III

ONCE THE shutters had been put up and the doors locked for the night, the prisoners were at the mercy of their guards. A turn of a switch could transform the already dimly lit messes into a series of gloomy caves where shadowy figures huddled round evil-smelling goon lamps. Reading, writing, drawing, handicrafts were abandoned when the lights went out, and only the most elementary form of cooking could be attempted. The prisoners reverted to the habits of their forebears and sat around telling one another stories until the lights came on again.

While the lights were on the room was always throbbing with conversation, a steady murmur punctuated at intervals by bursts of laughter, snatches of song and the persistent tap-tap of the handyman who was making a frying-pan or drinking mug out of old tin cans. In each of the twelve cells of this enormous hive eight men fed, played, argued, worked, shouted, dreamed or ate out their hearts in loneliness. Over everything hung a pall of tobacco smoke, the warm fug of drying clothes, the smell of cooking.

To Peter, as he lay on his bunk waiting for his turn to use the cooking stove and listening to Loveday's voice droning away at some long and involved argument, it seemed reasonable that there should be only six men in their mess. Loveday was more than equal to three normal men. During the daytime, when they could separate and wander to different parts of the compound, it was not too bad. If they passed him on the circuit they were not compelled to talk. They could say hallo the first time they met, and after that they could pretend not to notice him. At mealtimes it was bad, because then there was no escape; but in the evenings, when they were locked in for the night, it was becoming impossible.

The others were easy to live with. They were men who could immerse themselves in what they were doing, like Saunders with his strange inventions, or Otto with his memories, or even like Hugo with his desire to preserve the niceties of social life. They could all sit for hours with their personalities wrapped up inside them like a cat sitting within the circle of its tail. He thought of John sitting for hours completely absorbed in a book. If he looked down now he would see him, pliant and graceful, his long black hair and fringe of fluffy beard; a young tramp dressed in all the clothes he possessed, a blanket round his shoulders, two pairs of socks inside his wooden clogs. Silent. If he spoke to him, said, "What d'you think of this, John? Is the perspective right?" he would look up and say, "What, old boy?"—coming back to earth—"What did you say?" And he would answer; give enough of himself to answer the question, and then withdraw himself again. Most of the prisoners were like that. In most messes there would be long periods of silence. They had said so much to each other, knew one another so well, that they could be happy retired within themselves.

But Loveday was not like that. He could not curl up within himself, he had to be arguing all the time. He had to prove himself. The sight of the others curled within the protective circles of their tails was a challenge to drag them out. He would fling a controversial statement into the silence of the mess, throw it out addressed to no one in particular, as a fisherman casts a fly across a silent pool; and before long an argument would be raging, a stupid argument without a point, like the one that was raging now. He was full of the mumbo-jumbo of psychology. He would remember things the others had said several days before, and which had slipped their memory. He would use these words to prove that they were not normal, would talk in elaborate parables and attempt to psycho-analyse them. There was no peace with Loveday.

When Hugo and Saunders argued, as they often did, the argument was for Hugo and Saunders, and would go unheeded by the others. But for Loveday the argument was not for himself and the other fellow; it was for him and the whole mess. He could not rest unless the whole mess was involved. With the other arguments, one could ride them out, work on and let the argument pass over one's head; but there was an insistent quality in Loveday's voice that made this impossible when he was talking. The voice was addressed to all the people who were still outside the argument, and in the end it was impossible to resist. After a while they had become more cautious, and when the fly was flicked across the pool the fish refused to rise. Then, after a while, he began to address individual members of the mess. Their only defence was to be doing something —reading, writing, or drawing. Then they could say, "Look, old boy, I'm busy," or "Don't interrupt me for a moment, Loveday, I think I've got it now," or even "For Christ's sake shut up, Loveday—can't you see I'm busy!" But even this was not sufficient defence, for as soon as two of them started to talk he would join in, and before long the whole mess would be involved in Loveday's argument.

Peter looked at his watch. It was time for him to take over the stove, and he could escape into the kitchen at the end of the block. He carried with him some pieces of wood that he had stolen from the theatre, and the already half-cooked pie.

The kitchen was filled with smoke, and in darkness. He groped for the switch and turned it on.

"PUT OUT THAT LIGHT!"

The earlier cook was just taking his dinner off the stove. "I had to put the light out," he explained. "The chimney leaks, and I had to open the black-out to let the smoke escape. Bloody sentry put a bullet in here the other night because we had a light showing."

When he had gone, Peter closed the black-out shutters and switched on the light. The top of the stove was covered with tins of all sizes—poachers. He pushed them to one side, put the salmon pie on the ring, stoked up the fire, switched off the light, and dashed for the window, almost asphyxiated.

Someone opened the door and switched on the light.

"PUT OUT THAT LIGHT!"

The visitor switched the light off again, and Peter replaced the black-out shutters. "All right—you can come in now."

He was a short, round man with carefully parted hair and a blanket worn as a cloak across his shoulders. He carried a Klim tin full of water. "Got any room for a pisser?" he asked.

"Look for yourself," Peter said.

The man looked and said he'd call back later.

Peter switched off the light and opened the shutters again, but soon the stove needed refuelling and he dashed back into the smoke to add more wood. His half-hour stooge was a nightmare of darkness, smoke and burning pie; until at last he staggered proudly back to the mess, pie prepared, to tell John that the stove was free for frying the biscuits.

"I was talking to old Bandy this afternoon," Saunders said through a mouthful of pie. "He had a letter from an aunt saying that his wife was going round with an American."

"Better than a Pole—eh, Otto?" Hugo said.

Otto grinned.

"As it happens he knows all about it," Saunders continued. "She wrote and told him. The chap's married, with two kids."

"That wouldn't make me any happier," Hugo said.

"But why couldn't she mind her own business?" Peter said. "What can Bandy do about it, anyway?"

"Ah, that's just it." Saunders had already finished his pie. "Better not to know. I bet she's a spinster."

"Who?"

"The aunt. She'd find something better to write about if she was married."

"The same applies to mine," Hugo said. "All she thinks about is her damned cat. She's as rich as Crœsus and, d'you know, she goes and stands in a queue for hours every day for cat's-meat for the wretched animal. Still"—he brightened—"she isn't spending much."

Peter finished his pie, and went to relieve John at the stove. He found him talking to the man with the Klim tin.

"You go and eat your pie," Peter said. "I'll finish the biscuits."

"I've done three," John said. "I opened the window in the washhouse, it creates a draught." He put the three biscuits that he had fried on to a metal dish. "I'll take these with me. This chap wants to get on as early as possible."

"I'm trying to make a cake," the stranger explained. "We've got a birthday next week."

"Won't be long," Peter told him. He put the last of the wood on the fire, and set to work to fry the damp biscuits in Red Cross margarine.

"How's the new show going?" the stranger asked.

"Should be pretty good," Peter said. "It's a light-hearted kind of thing, a sort of burlesque melodrama."

"That's the sort of thing we want—we have too many tragedies. *Gaslight*, *Hamlet*—that sort of thing. What we want is a laugh."

"We're doing *A Midsummer Night's Dream* in the spring. They're going to try to get old Saunders from our mess to play Bottom—he's a natural."

"That chap Loveday in your mess is a bit odd, isn't he?"

"He's all right," Peter said.

"He stopped me on the circuit the other day and told me that I had a definite aura. I wonder what the hell he meant? He was off before I could say a word."

"It's his sense of humour," Peter said.

When he had cleared the dinner things away his stooge for the day was done. John would make the late evening brew, and the dirty mugs would not be washed up until the morning. Thankfully he climbed on to his top bunk to finish a sketch he was making of the long room with its rows of identical messes; identical in shape but individual in content and arrangement.

Usually he enjoyed sitting up there near the ceiling, listening to the ever-repeated pattern of life in the room below; but this evening the tightness inside him that had been there since he had received his mother's letter prevented him from working. He sat there listlessly. In the end mess John read a book while Loveday, Otto, Hugo and Saunders began a rubber of bridge.

CHAPTER IV

ON HIS way to the camp theatre the next morning, Peter saw Otto walking alone, hands in pockets, round the circuit.

"Hallo, Otto. How's the hole going?"

Otto looked at him sharply.

"John told me," Peter said.

"It goes well enough."

"When d'you think you'll be out?"

"In a month—perhaps two."

"Where are you making for—the Baltic?"

"I shall go to Warsaw," Otto said. "I do not think it is possible to get to England. In Warsaw I shall fight underground."

"What are the others doing?"

"I do not know about the others."

"Is there any chance of getting in, d'you think?"

Otto smiled. "I really do not think so. There are so many now. The nearer we get to finishing, the more there are who have places. There are now thirty of us."

"Where do you come?" Peter asked.

"I am third. There is a man, I do not say his name, who has offered me a thousand pounds for my place."

"A thousand quid! That's expensive digging."

"I do not dig for money," Otto said.

"No, of course not."

They walked for some time in silence, while Peter cursed himself for asking if there was any chance of getting in. At this stage, when all the work was done. "How did you get started?" he asked.

"Started?"

"In the escape game—how did you first get into a scheme?"

"First I escape from Poland," Otto said. "I go to Constanza and there I get a ship to Marseilles. In France I join the French Air Force, because I am already a pilot. I train in France, and while I am still training the Germans come. So I go to Orăn and Casablanca. From there I go to Gibraltar and to England. In England, I train again. I train for a long time, and then I fly and I am shot down."

"So when you get back to Warsaw you complete the circuit."

"Yes, I complete the circuit. And I do not go away again. I do more good at home, I think."

"What I meant was, how did you get into the escaping game here in the camp?" Peter said. "It seems a pretty closed shop to me."

"That is because you are late arriving," Otto said. "Now you must start a scheme of your own. All the prisoners of experience are banded together. There is not room for anyone who is not experienced like themselves."

"You can say that again," Peter said. "It's all very well to say start a scheme of your own, but all the possible starting places have been exhausted." He did not trust the possibility of Tyson's tunnel. He believed in having as many irons in the fire as he could.

"You will have to think . . . Perhaps when you are moved to a new camp . . ."

"D'you think we shall be?"

"I have been in four camps already. They do not believe in keeping us in one place for very long." Otto took his hand from his pocket and with a quick flick of his wrist threw a small parcel through the wire into the Russian compound. One of the Russians, a skeleton dressed in rags, made a quick dive at it and thrust it inside his coat.

"What was that?"

"Bread," Otto said.

"But we already give up part of our rations to feed the Russians."

"That is given to the Russians who work. The men who are too ill to work get nothing. One of them died some time ago, and they kept his body in the hut three weeks before they told the guards."

"Good God!"

"They drew his rations. You English do not realise. You say the German is not too bad. Perhaps he is not—to you. You have the Red Cross, and you have many German prisoners. Do you think that the nations who have not these threats are treated in the same way as you? You do not know the Germans. You are blind in your own shell of "good sport." You English are so bloody sporting that you shame the Germans into treating you also sporting. But you could not do it without the strength behind you. The Russians do not have Red Cross parcels—no, they are treated like pigs——" Otto stopped himself. "I am sorry. You will think that I am fanatic. But it is true, what I tell you."

"I've heard that the Russians don't treat the German prisoners too well," Peter said. "Perhaps if they treated their prisoners decently the Germans would do the same."

"It is not a matter of treating decently!" Otto shouted. "What would you do without your parcels from England? Could you live on the German ration?"

"No."

"Then do not talk of treating decently!"

What is the use of talking at all, Peter thought. What is the use of trying to generalise. He thought back over his captivity, of the friendly, decent Germans who had been his guards and captors. Little men, men with a sense of humour, caught up in the vast machine of their own making which had got beyond their power to control. Then he thought of Otto and his torture at the hands of the *Gestapo*.

Of the Russian prisoners, starved, worked to death, hoarding their dead for the extra rations. The concentration camps. The prisoners there were Germans themselves. They did not have Red Cross parcels. What would he and the others be like without them? How would they behave?

They came round by the Russian compound again. The smell of the huts was strong, even out here in the open air; a sharp, acrid odour, with a cloying, almost sweet aftertaste—like the smell of the monkey-house at the Zoo. There were some torn thin blankets hanging on a line, and in sheltered corners of the compound queer thin figures with large heads and dirty drawn faces sat nodding in the late winter sunshine.

Down on the football pitch there was a rugger match between Block 3 and Block 5. The teams were cheered on by their supporters, who formed a thick margin all round the pitch. At the sound of cheering borne by the wind the nodding figures in the Russian compound looked up as though in wonderment.

"I should like to talk to you about Alan," Otto said.

"What about him?"

"You find him difficult, I think."

"He's a bit of a nuisance at times."

"It is not his fault," Otto said. "He has a good heart."

"I don't doubt it. But you need more than a good heart in a place like this, as you know well enough. If he'd only give it a rest at times."

"He is unhappy, you know."

"So are a lot of other chaps."

"It does not help to tease him," Otto said. "It will only make him worse."

"I don't tease him—I keep away from him as much as I can."

"The others tease him," Otto said. "You have some influence with the others. Perhaps you will persuade them."

"It does him good, I think. If you don't rag the man he'll get worse and worse."

"I do not think so. He is very lonely."

"What do you want us to do—talk psychology?" Peter felt a distinct aversion to this lobbying on Loveday's behalf; perhaps it was the flattery of Otto's assumption that he had influence over the others.

"He should not be here," Otto said. "He should be in the hospital."

"Come off it—he's not as bad as that."

"He is very unhappy," Otto said. "It is understanding that he needs. I do not like to think what he will do when I am gone."

"Haven't you told him that you're in the *abort* scheme?"

"I have not told him, because we may not succeed. Their is no point in hurting him without cause."

"You will tell him, though?"

"If we succeed I shall tell him the night before we leave. If we fail, then he need not know."

"You pander to him too much," Peter said.

"I know him," Otto said. "I do not think it is a good thing to tease. Understanding will help him more than teasing."

"But he won't co-operate," Peter was suddenly impatient with Otto because of Loveday. "I asked him to help me with the scenery once, but he said he had no time for such childish activities. He doesn't seem to want to co-operate . . . That reminds me, I promised Bandy I'd go down there this morning. I must get along."

The camp theatre was in the White House, and when Peter arrived Bandy Beecham was in the middle of a rehearsal. The chorus, complete with long flaxen wigs and built-up brassières, were shaking the floor as they "Can-Canned" furiously up and down the flimsy stage.

"Stop!" Bandy said. "Stop! I can't bear it." He put his

hand to his forehead. "How many times have I told you? Lightly, lightly—remember you're supposed to be young ladies. And you, Rowe—tighten up that brassière a bit. It looks indecent."

Peter's scenery was behind the stage and he took advantage of the lull to walk across. "How's it going, Bandy?"

"Fine, fine, old boy. Will you have those flats finished by to-morrow?"

"Providing you don't alter it again."

"That's all right—it's fine now," Bandy told him. "Just the job . . . Now, girls, let's run through once more—then we'll do the seduction scene."

Peter fetched his brushes from where he had hidden them under the stage, and began to mix his colours. He was painting the backcloth and wings for the baronial hall scene—panelled walls with plenty of scope for trick perspective. He enjoyed painting scenery. There was something in the large scale of the drawing, the wide sweep of the brush, that gave him a measure of release. He enjoyed making water colours of the camp and pencil sketches of life inside the barrack block. He enjoyed the rugger matches when captivity was forgotten in the dominating urge to get the ball across the line. But none of these gave him quite the satisfaction that he found in painting scenery. Perhaps it was the very falseness of it all, the glamour that coloured the production of even the camp theatre shows, that made him forget his present surroundings and lose himself in the scene that he was painting.

While he lined-out the panels of carved woodwork he listened to the high-spirited and bawdy wooing of the village maiden by the dark and fiercely amorous lord of the manor, who was played by Tyson. The maiden, almost Teutonic in her blonde and buxom charm, was importuned in rhyming couplets by her ardent admirer, sinister behind black handle-bar moustaches. First she backed nervously towards the footlights, then suddenly darting to the very front of the stage screamed in a confidential aside to her imaginary audience:

> *If I say 'yes' he'll be content*
> *But what a way to pay the rent!*"

He had heard it several times before, but each time it made him laugh. It seemed to him as he worked that this ribaldry expressed the irrepressible spirit that would carry a tunnel beyond the wire, that baited the guards at the expense of personal comfort. Wryly he wondered how much of that spirit depended on the Red Cross parcels.

It was nearly lunchtime when John came to fetch him and while Peter was cleaning his brushes Tyson came across to them.

"You two still keen on the cookhouse job?"

"Yes," John said.

"Meeting in my room this afternoon," Tyson told them. "Come straight along as soon as you've finished lunch."

As they walked past the hospital towards the barrack block Peter told John of his conversation with Otto, about Loveday.

"Ragging's just what he needs," John said, "take him out of himself."

"That's exactly what I said, but Otto doesn't agree."

"Loveday's got too many sharp corners," John said. "They need wearing down a bit, that's all. Otto's too easy with him."

Peter did not reply.

"I wonder how far they'd got with the cookhouse tunnel before they had to abandon it," John said. "I wonder if we'll get out before Otto."

"They couldn't have got very far or they'd have carried on," Peter said. "They'd never abandon a tunnel that was nearly finished."

"We'll be out before the washhouse chaps anyway," John said. "They haven't even cut through the concrete yet."

They found Loveday wrestling with *A Textbook of Psychology* and Hugo asleep on his bunk. Both Saunders and Otto were out of the mess but by the window stood the inevitable stooge from the washhouse tunnel. Ever since the work had been started there had been a stooge at their window, the only one which gave a good view of the path which the Germans would have to use to reach the barrack block. Yesterday Peter had been irritated by the silent obsessed figure which stood, blocking the light and over-hearing all their conversation, peering sideways out of the window, making their mess a public property. Now, warmed by the thought of their own tunnel, he asked the stooge how the work was going.

"Dunno," the man said. "I've never seen it. I expect it's getting on all right." He turned furtively back to the window.

"I'll go for the hot water," John said. "You stay and collect the soup." He took the metal jug from the shelf and set out for the cookhouse.

Saunders came in. "Soup up yet?"

"Not yet," Peter said.

"It's up in Block 2." He sat disconsolately on one of the bunks waiting for his lunch. He got up restlessly and crossed to where Peter was setting out the table. "What's the conscription age for women, Pete?"

"God knows." Peter said.

"It's my old woman." Saunders picked up one of the forks and started prodding holes in the table top. "I can't make out whether she's joining the W.A.A.F. because she's got to, or if she's fed up with staying at home."

"How old is she?"

"Thirty."

"Probably called up," Peter said. "She'll be better off in the W.A.A.F. than in a factory."

"I suppose so." Saunders placed the fork carefully back in position and walked to the door of the mess. "This soup's a bloody long time coming to-day." He began to pick idly with his fingernail at a splinter which projected from the side of his wooden bunk, until the soup arrived in a galvanised iron dustbin carried by two of the British soldiers who worked as orderlies in the cookhouse. There were about a dozen of these men who boiled the morning tea water in huge cauldrons and made the midday soup with the meagre German rations. They dumped the dustbin in the corridor where it was taken over by the barrack messing officer. "Soup up!" he shouted. "SOUP!"

Peter joined the queue of stooges in the central corridor. Each man carried a pile of eight basins. As each stooge reached the head of the queue he shouted out the number of his mess and his fellow prisoners came to collect the bowls into which the soup, evil-smelling and dark green in colour, was slopped by the messing officer.

Hugo had found a piece of meat in his soup and when Peter brought in the last two bowls the others were trying to identify it.

"I think it's horse-meat," Hugo said.

"Dead Russian," said Saunders.

"I shouldn't joke," Loveday said. "We found a cat in it once."

"Probably a rabbit," Hugo suggested.

"I know a cat from a rabbit," Loveday said. "Since when did a rabbit have claws?"

"Let's not talk about it." Hugo decided he was not hungry and pushed his bowl to the centre of the table.

"Aren't you going to finish that?" Saunders asked.

Hugo pushed the bowl towards him.

"Gash soup! GASH SOUP! GASH SOUP!!" It was the messing officer shouting from the corridor. There was a rush of stooges to collect their share of the surplus soup.

John came back with half a bowlful. They drew lots for it, and Loveday won.

"What's for dinner to-night?" Saunders asked, finishing the last of Hugo's soup.

"Salmon pie," Peter said. "Come on, step on it." He wanted to get the washing-up done so that they could go to Tyson's meeting.

"What, again? We had salmon pie yesterday."

"We had two lots of salmon this week."

"O.K.," Saunders said. "Try to pep it up a bit more this time. What's all the hurry about—anyone would think you were going to the flicks or something."

The meeting had started when they arrived, and they squeezed in behind a dozen or so prisoners who had crowded into Tyson's mess at the end of the room. "Well, that's the first two teams," he was saying, "all men with experience. We shall work two shifts and when these chaps have had enough we can ring a change with one of the dispersal teams. That means we'll need two dispersal squads and two complete sets of stooges."

Peter and John found themselves in one of the stooging teams.

"Now—just a brief outline of the scheme." Tyson sounded enthusiastic. "It's to be in the central cookhouse, under one of the boilers which is no longer used. It's an old tunnel that we had to abandon last autumn because of water seepage. I went down myself yesterday, and it seems to have dried out quite a bit. There have been one or two small falls but I reckon we can shore it up and get it working again. Now I don't want anyone to come in with any false illusions. As I say, it's a derelict tunnel and we abandoned it because it wasn't considered safe. We may work for months and then find we have to give it up again. But that's up to you.

"The next problem is how to get the excavated clay away from the tunnel—that usually *is* the difficulty. Stewart's lot are lucky in that respect because their dispersal is right on their doorstep as it were. So are the chaps who are using our washroom—not that I think they'll get very far. Now in our case we shall utilise the fact that stooges go to the cookhouse every morning and lunchtime to fetch the tea water. The clay from the tunnel will be carried away in the water jugs."

"What about the morning tea?" someone asked.

"I was coming to that. At present each stooge collects about half a jugful of tea. In future every alternate mess will collect a full jug of tea, which will be shared with the mess next door. The stooge from that mess will collect a jugful of clay."

"It'll never work." It was the same small dark man who had spoken before.

"Why not?"

"Suppose they don't wash the jugs out?"

"They can keep the jugs separate, and use the same one for the clay each time."

"I don't think the chaps would agree to that," the dark man said.

"Nonsense, of course they will. By doing that we can take out as much clay as we like. The guards are used to seeing a constant stream of men with jugs at mealtimes. The earth will be brought straight back here and then we can disperse it at our leisure. It's a perfectly watertight scheme."

There was a roar of laughter, at which Tyson looked surprised. Then he saw the joke. "Perhaps foolproof would have been better than watertight—although foolproof is a bit too strong with some of you chaps around." He looked pleased, as though he had scored a point.

"How shall we get the wood for shoring into the cookhouse without being spotted?" someone asked.

"Firewood for the boiler. Any more questions?"

"Yes—when do we start?"

"Early next week. We're just making a new frame for

M

the trap, and getting the stooging system organised. We want to work it so that we don't get too many chaps coming in with their jugs at the same time—and not too few. Everything must go on exactly as it always does."

"How far have they already dug?" John asked.

"About a hundred feet—there's still a long way to go. But if everything goes smoothly we should break sometime in the spring."

"Where will it come up?" Peter asked.

"We're going under the Russian compound. It's under their wire already. I have considered coming up and making a dispersal under their huts—but I don't altogether trust 'em. We'll do it if we have to but at the moment the intention is to cut straight through and come up on the other side of the main road. Any more questions?"

There were no more questions.

"Right," Tyson said. "The first team will meet here at nine o'clock on Monday morning."

CHAPTER V

FOR THE next few weeks Peter and John did little more for the cookhouse tunnel than they had done for Stewart in the *abort dienst*. They stooged on draughty corners, stood for hours looking out of windows or sat propped against the wall of the White House counting the Germans as they came in and out through the compound gates. But now they had a place in the tunnel, even if they were only thirty-two and thirty-three on the list, and the stooging had more purpose.

As Tyson had foreseen, the digging teams were forced to spend a considerable time in strengthening the shoring and repairing damage to the tunnel walls before they could start to push their way towards the wire. As time went on Peter and John listened to his reports with diminishing hope; it seemed that they would never begin to move.

But their spirits rose again as a number of their fellow stooges and some of the dispersal team, unable to stand this period of frustration and delay, dropped out. Slowly, place by place, they began to move up the list towards a place in the digging team.

When digging finally started in earnest, they spent most of their time as members of a dispersal gang, bringing the clay to the barrack block in the water jugs and packing it into small bags made from shirts and underclothes. They took some of these bags, suspended round their necks under their coats by a piece of string, to the *aborts*, and disposed of their contents in the usual way. The rest of the bags they hid under the bunks, and in the short interval between dusk and lock-up they buried the clay they held in the ground outside the huts. It was slow, tedious, uninteresting work, but it was one stage better than stooging.

Then, one afternoon as they were finishing their lunch, Tyson came into the mess. "You two all right for a spell below this afternoon?"

"On the ball," John said.

"Right. Come to the cookhouse as soon as you can. Wear your tunnelling kit under your ordinary clothes, and bring a handkerchief or something for your heads." He went out, leaving behind him an awkward silence, which was broken by Saunders.

"You didn't tell us you were on a *dienst*," he said. "How long has this been going on?"

"Oh, not long," Peter said, minimising it. "We haven't much chance of getting out, I'm afraid—we're not in the first ten."

"It's all a stupid waste of time," Loveday said. "Why don't you individuals settle down? Settle down and study like I do. I'm improving my mind." He tapped a finger on his forehead. "It's a natural psychological reaction to want to escape. When an individual is locked up he wants to get out. You ought to overcome it. Look at Otter here—he doesn't waste his time trying to escape, he's an old kriegie. Eh, Otter?" He poked Otto in the ribs with a large raw finger. "We old kriegies don't try to escape, do we, Otter? We study and improve our minds."

Peter looked at Otto, who smiled and shrugged his shoulders.

"How did you two manage to get in?" Saunders glanced at John engrossed in his book again. "Why pick on you two of all people?"

John looked up; innocent. "Well, as a matter of fact, they spotted that we were outstandingly good tough types, and asked us if we'd run the tunnel for them."

"Good types!" Loveday shouted. "There's conceit for you. Good types indeed! Nothing but read, read, read. Because we're not good enough to talk to, I suppose. Captain Clinton has to withdraw himself from the others. Good types indeed——"

"He was only joking, Alan," Otto said it gently. "He didn't really mean it."

"Then he should say what he means," Loveday said. "All this double-dealing and cross-talk. How can an individual live in peace while all this deceit is in the air? Why didn't you two tell us you were in a tunnel?"

"Didn't think you'd be particularly interested." Peter was hurriedly getting their football clothes out of the locker.

"So you didn't think I'd be interested, eh? What d'you think I am, eh? So you think I'm not loyal to the mess—you think——"

"Come on." Peter threw John's bundle across to where he was sitting. "Time we were going down, John."

"O.K., chum." John put his book on the shelf above his bed and began to change into his tunnelling clothes.

The scene in the central cookhouse reminded Peter of the setting for a modern ballet. The four boilers, like enormous witches' cauldrons, stood side by side on an apron of concrete against the farthest wall. Beneath the end boiler, now dead, was the narrow entrance to the tunnel, open; and by its side lay the trapdoor made from concrete in a shallow wooden tray. In each of the side walls small high windows threw their spotlights on to the figures of the orderlies, who tended the boilers, and the early shift of tunnellers, who had just come to the surface. The tunnellers were dressed in woollen undervests and long pants, patched like harlequins, bright yellow from the puddled clay. On their heads they wore woollen caps or handkerchiefs knotted at the corners and, dancer-like, they wore no shoes.

Tyson, already in his tunnelling clothes, was waiting for them. "Hurry up, chaps," he said.

Peter and John quickly took off their outer clothing and

joined the new shift, who were waiting to go below. It was cold and they shivered as Tyson slid under the boiler and, after much grunting and straining, disappeared from view. Peter, following, found a hole in the floor about two feet square. There was a rough ladder fixed to the side of the shaft at the bottom of which the flickering rays of a lamp showed Tyson's legs as he crawled out of sight. Presently his face appeared where his legs had been. "Go easy down the ladder," he said.

At the bottom of the shaft was a square chamber about six feet by four in which a man crouched, working a crude concertina-like air pump made from a canvas kit-bag. By his side the goon lamp cast its lurid glow across his sweating face as he swung to the rhythm of the creaking pump. The walls and ceiling of the chamber and the mouth of the tunnel which opened from it were of solid wood, bed-boards jammed together side by side; but the floor was liquid clay.

Tyson was crouching half in and half out of the tunnel. In his hands he had two smoking lamps, one of which he passed to Peter. "Follow me!" He spoke in a whisper, as though he could be heard through twelve feet of solid earth.

The tunnel, once they had left the chamber, was no longer lined with wood. The walls and ceiling dripped with water which gathered in long puddles on the floor and, as he wriggled after Tyson into the blackness, Peter felt this water soak through his woollen vest and grip him with its icy fingers.

After crawling for about fifteen feet the light in front stopped moving, and when Peter caught up with it he found Tyson crouching over a hole in the tunnel floor, about three feet from where it came to an abrupt end. "It goes down another six feet," he whispered. "The real tunnel starts from the bottom of this shaft. The upper tunnel is only a dummy. We camouflage the trapdoor over this shaft whenever we leave it, and then if the goons discover the upper tunnel

they'll think it ends here. They'll just fill in the top shaft
and this bit of tunnel—and then when the flap's all over we
can strike the lower tunnel from another shaft. That way
we only lose the short upper tunnel, and save the lower one."
He chuckled and climbed down the second ladder into the
lower gallery.

Peter, stifling his feeling of panic, followed. This was
what he had wanted. He'd got the chance, and now he must
go through with it.

It seemed deep, deep down in the earth. Somehow the
second shaft seemed a hundred times deeper than the first.
It seemed completely beyond help from the surface. At
intervals, where there had been a fall, patches of wooden
shoring bulged ominously inwards. He had to fight hard
to force himself to carry on.

He seemed to have been crawling for about half an hour
before he again caught up with Tyson, who had reached the
end of the tunnel. "You work here," Tyson told him.
"Here's a knife. Put the clay you dig out into this toboggan."
He showed Peter a rough wooden trough about eighteen
inches long by twelve inches wide. "When you pull the rope
twice I'll haul it back to the lower shaft. I pass it up to the
top tunnel, and Clinton will send it back to the upper shaft
in another toboggan. You see now why we need such a
large team."

When Tyson had left him there was silence; more complete silence than Peter had ever known. It seemed as
though the eighteen feet of soil above his head was pressing
down, pressing inwards. Then, in the silence, he heard the
faint hiss of air pushed by the man at the pump through its
life-line of jam tins joined end to end. This metal pipe,
coming along the upper tunnel, down the shaft and along
the wall of the lower tunnel, was his connection with the
outside world—that, and the rope which pulled the toboggan.
He took the knife and began to hack away at the clay in
front of him.

An hour later Tyson called a halt. John took Peter's place at the head of the tunnel, while Peter pulled the clay back to the lower shaft. The rope, thinly plaited from the sisal string off the Red Cross parcels, cut deeply into his hands, and the strain of pulling the heavy toboggan through the thick sludge of the tunnel floor made his shoulders ache. He had blisters on the palms of his hands from the handle of the knife and, as he unloaded the clay into jam tins and passed them up to Tyson at the top of the shaft, he began to realise that there was more to tunnelling than he had thought.

At the end of the two-hour shift they came to the surface. Peter knew now why the earlier tunnellers had staggered as they crossed the kitchen floor. He had been sweating for the last two hours, and his woollen underclothes were wringing wet with sweat and moisture from the tunnel.

The stooges had a hot bath waiting for them; a real, galvanised iron bath. Peter had not known that such a thing existed in the camp. As he sat in the luxury of the warm and muddy water, he began to think that perhaps tunnelling was worth while after all.

As the tunnel moved steadily on towards the wire the possibility of escape loomed larger and larger in Peter's mind. He still played football for his block, still painted scenery for the theatre, talked on the circuit and made sketches of his fellow prisoners; but always at the back of his mind was the tunnel. From waking until sleeping he carried with him the warm comforting thought of that long, dark, slippery, suffocating burrow that would, one day, take him and John under the barbed wire and away to that free, now almost unreal world that lay beyond. Whenever he walked along the path between the cookhouse and the Russian compound he knew that he was walking over the tunnel, remembered lying there and hearing the footsteps walking as he was walking now.

He enjoyed working at the tunnel face. Lying flat on his stomach, picking away unseeing at the clay in front of his head, he felt that he was really getting somewhere, really doing something towards getting out of the camp. Moreover he was alone, lying there in the darkness and dank air of the tunnel: alone in a small world of silence, a world bounded by the feeble rays of the lamp that guttered by his head. He was more alone than he could be anywhere else in the camp. Up there in the crowded barrack block, on the teeming circuit, he was aware all the time of his fellow prisoners; their habits of speech and the almost maddening physical proximity—the body odour and the unconscious elbow in the ribs. But down in the tunnel it was dark and lonely, and he sang to himself as he picked away at the hard clay, and felt sorry when it was his turn to leave the loneliness of the tunnel to go back to his place in the shaft.

One evening, after they had been locked in for the night, he and John sat on John's bunk talking in low voices about the tunnel.

"It's funny," Peter said, "it's almost like going to a woman." He laughed, conscious of a slight embarrassment. "I get a sort of peace down there—the peace you get from a woman."

"Sort of symbolism?" John said.

"I don't know, it may be. It's certainly not entirely because we're getting out—it's the tunnel itself. It's a sort of retreat, almost like burrowing back into the womb. Sounds silly, I expect. You'll think I'm going round the bend."

"This is the bend round which we twain are met," John said.

Peter laughed. "Does it get you like that?"

"I'd rather have a woman," John said.

Suddenly Loveday interrupted them. "I know what you're talking about," he shouted. "You're talking about me. You're always talking about me. Why can't you mind your own business?"

Peter looked up in astonishment. "Don't be damn' silly —it was nothing to do with you."

"What was it about then? Why do we have to have secrets in the mess?"

"It was nothing to do with you," Peter said.

"Clinton kept glancing at me, I saw him."

"I was looking at you because you were breathing so heavily," John said. "I thought you were going to faint or something."

"He was doing his Yogi," Saunders said.

"You're very clever, Clinton," Loveday said. "You're all very clever." He looked round wildly. "But I can defend myself. You won't get away with it, you know. I'm well aware of what it's all about."

"That's all right then," Peter said. "Let's drop it, shall we?"

"Very convenient," Loveday said. "A very easy way out."

He relapsed into gloomy silence, a silence which grew more and more strained.

"Let us have an early brew," Otto suggested. "It is nearly nine o'clock. The jug has been on the stove since six."

No one replied.

"Good show. I go to see if it has boiled yet." He was about to leave the room when the lights went out. "We must now wait for the cocoa." He lit the lamp instead.

"Come on, Saunders," Hugo said. "It's your turn to tell a story. And mind it's a good sexy one."

"Shall I tell you about the binge we had in Montreal?" Saunders suggested.

"Make it snappy then," Hugo said. "Cut out all the irrelevancies."

"O.K. Come in close—I don't want the chaps next door to hear."

They gathered round the flickering lamp while Saunders,

grotesque in his balaclava helmet and cut-down greatcoat, began his story.

"It was while I was training in Canada." He brushed his moustache upwards with the back of his hand. "Well—it was when I'd finished training really. At least, I hadn't really finished. We were on our way to Gunnery School. We'd failed the Navigation part of it. . . . No, it wasn't— I'm wrong there. It was *after* we'd finished Gunnery School and were on our way to England——"

"Does it matter?" Hugo asked.

"Well—you want me to get the story right, don't you?"

"That's right, Saunders," John said. "You take your time."

"Well, it's a long time since it happened, and a lot of things have happened since it happened."

"All right," Hugo said. "Sorry I spoke."

"Are we right now?" Saunders asked.

"Yes, yes, yes."

"Well. It was in Montreal anyway. I remember that because all the signs were in French. There were a lot of horse-drawn carriages in the streets, and someone told me that some of the people there couldn't speak English. . . . Not that any of them could really, not King's English—but these couldn't speak English at all."

"Extraordinary," Hugo murmured.

"Everyone should be able to speak English," John said solemnly.

"That's what I told them. Fancy a city in the middle of Canada, and half the people can't speak English!"

"We'll start a mission after the war," John said. "Teaching English to the Canadians. We'll make Saunders president."

"Let him get on with the story," Peter said.

"Well, it's no good if they don't speak English," Hugo said.

"Well—she said she didn't," Saunders said. "She may have been imported from France for all I know."

"Suppose you start at the beginning," John suggested.

"Well. I was in Montreal——"

The lights came on.

"All right, I'll save it," Saunders said. "They're bound to go out again before the evening's finished."

"In the interval I will make the cocoa," Otto said.

"He's the only adult among the lot of you," Loveday said when Otto had left the mess. "You're a lot of kids."

There was a short silence, no one wanted to start an argument. Then the lights went out again.

"Come on, Saunders," Peter said. "What about getting on with that story?"

"Righto." Saunders lit the lamp. "Gather round again, chaps—come on, Loveday. Now, how far had I got?"

"You were in Montreal," Peter reminded him.

"Ah, yes. Well—we'd just stopped off for a few hours on our way to Halifax. We were going back to England. Or were we? Perhaps we'd just finished our Navigation Course——"

"We've had all that," John said. "You were in Montreal and they didn't speak English."

"Oh, yes—we'd had to change a train or something. Anyway, there we were in Montreal with nothing to do for an hour or two."

"Heaven!" Hugo said. "How lovely to have nothing to do for an hour or two."

"Come on, Saunders," Peter said.

"Well, as I said, there were a lot of these horse-drawn carriages, things like big prams but drawn by horses—you know the sort of thing. So we stopped one and told him to take us round the town. The horse had a sort of white loose cover over its ears with red tassels on 'em——"

"Jolly useful in a place like this," John said.

"Shut up, John."

"The driver was as old as the hills," Saunders went on, "older than God almost—and he whipped the horse into a sort of shambling trot and off we went, smart as ninepence. I never was much of a one for looking at buildings, but it was quite good fun sitting in an open carriage looking at all the people on the streets. It was a warm sunny day, and the girls were in their summer frocks, and there were awnings out over the pavements in front of the shops. We went up to the top of Mount Royal—it's a sort of hill with a park on the top—and we looked at the city from there. Then we came back into the town and had a look at the hill from down below. I was getting a bit dry by then, so I climbed up behind the driver and told him to take us somewhere where we could get a cup of tea."

"Typical Englishman," John said.

Saunders winked. "I think he must have thought that, because he leered at me. Dirty old devil he was too, with a bristly chin. He said, ' You want somewhere nice, eh?' ' Yes,' I said, ' take us to the best place in the town.' We'd had nothing to spend our money on in the prairie anyhow.

"Well, we left the town and got out somewhere in the residential districts. There were a lot of big houses like you get in Kensington. There weren't any shops there, and I began to wonder where the silly old fool was taking us. He stopped outside a damn' great house with columns outside and steps going up to the front door. ' Is this the place?' I said. ' Yes,' he said. Hell, I thought, this is going to cost a packet. ' What about it, chum?' I said.

"Old Dicky Hawthorne was with me, and he wasn't the sort of chap to back out. ' Tell him to wait,' he said, ' then if we don't like it we can cut off quick.'

"I told the cabby to wait and he just leered at me again. Familiar sort of chap he was—I could hear 'im chuckling as we walked up the steps.

"Well, we went up and rang the doorbell. I looked back at the cabby, and he'd pulled his hat over his eyes and gone to sleep. The door was opened by an old dame in black.

She must've been nearly as old as the cabby. She wore a black dress all covered with shiny black beads."

"Sequins," Hugo said.

"That's right—sort of spangles. But she was very dignified. She had a black velvet bow on the top of her head like my grandmother used to wear, and a crucifix on a long gold chain round her neck. She had ear-rings too. Now I come to think of it, I think she was made-up. I wouldn't be certain about that, but she certainly had class. I saluted—I hadn't got my commission then, I was a sergeant. ' Good afternoon,' I said, ' the driver brought us.' It was all I could think of to say."

"Very succinct," John said.

"Well, she drew us on one side, and took us into a sort of waiting-room off the side of the hall. It was all sort of modern, with red doors and plastic paint on the walls. There was chromium-plated furniture, easy-chairs with red covers, and the carpet was so thick that your feet sank into it like the foyer in the Gaumont. And the drawings on the walls!" He whistled. "What drawings! I've been round the Middle East a bit, but I've never seen drawings like that before. It was the rummiest set-up I ever saw." He stopped as the lights came on again.

"Go on," Peter said, "what happened then?"

"Ha, ha, no," Saunders said. "That's to be continued in our next."

"Come on," Peter said. "You've nearly finished."

"Haven't started yet," Saunders said. "You wait till the next time the lights go out."

"They will not go out again." Otto had come back with the jug of hot water. "There is a goon in the washhouse."

"You missed the second instalment of Saunders' story," Peter told him.

"Don't worry, it'll be tacked on to the beginning of the third," John said. "He has to get warmed up each time. Anyway, the lights'll go out again in a minute."

"I do not think so," Otto was serious.

"Why not?"

"The goon."

"You don't mean it," Peter said. "There isn't really a goon in the washhouse?"

"It is Hauptmann Mueller." Otto emptied half a packet of cocoa into the jug of hot water.

"What about the tunnel—they were working at it."

"He came in from the far end of the other block. Some chaps kept him talking while they got the trap down. Most of them are still down there, but they must remain there until he is gone. They could not risk having chaps covered in clay hanging around."

"Hope he doesn't stay long," John said.

"I wonder why he's here." Peter got to his feet. "We'd better hide those bags, John." He collected the dispersal bags from where they lay hidden among the tins and rubbish under Saunders' bunk. "What shall we do with them?"

Saunders made the usual suggestion, but no one laughed.

"Shove 'em down the lats," John said.

"Then we'll have to make some more."

"One man cannot search the whole block," Otto told them. "Put them back under the bunk, it will be all right."

"Goon in the block!" There was a sudden hush as the stooge called the conventional warning, unusual at this time of night.

"Come to tuck us up," someone shouted.

"Did you say *tuck*?"

They heard Stewart greet him as he entered the block. "Good evening, Herr Mueller. Dropped in for a brew?"

"Not this evening, thank you, Mr. Stewart." The German sounded preoccupied.

Peter went to the doorway of the mess and saw him standing in the corridor. He was alone. Slowly he began to walk down the room, looking into each mess as he passed.

"Looking for something, Herr Mueller?" someone asked.

What the hell's he want, Peter thought. Can they have got wind of something? If they raid the washhouse and find that tunnel, they're bound to search this block—and what about those bags? If we get sent to the cooler we'll lose our place in the cookhouse *dienst*. We shouldn't have left them here. It was damned careless. He went back and sat at the table.

Then Mueller was standing in the doorway of the mess.

"Good evening," Peter said.

The German came in without speaking. He was a sharp-nosed, pot-bellied man whose horn-rimmed spectacles magnified his pale blue eyes.

"Have a cup of cocoa, Mueller," Hugo rose to his feet, doing the honours.

"No, thank you." Mueller stood just inside the doorway, his thumbs hooked into the leather belt which supported his automatic pistol in its shabby holster. He was looking at the two "pin-up" girls pasted above Saunders' bunk. "That one is pleasing," he said. "This one—I do not like her so well. A little thin perhaps?"

Saunders was hurt. "Oh, I don't know. I'd rather sleep with her than with a policeman."

There was interest in Mueller's eyes. He looked at Saunders in disbelief. "*So?* In England is it not forbidden to sleep with policemen?"

Their laughter washed around his ears. He reddened, turned on his heels and marched out of the block.

"Now you've upset him," Hugo said.

"Hit him where it hurts the most, I expect," John said.

"Wonder he doesn't make a pass at you," Saunders said, "judging by the length of your hair."

"It *is* about time you had it cut, y'know." Hugo stroked his own immaculate head. "I must visit old Trumper when I get back. Jolly good barber, Trumper. You always come out with your hair longer than when you went in.

But controlled, of course—not down over your collar."

John made no reply, and Peter, knowing why he was growing his hair, changed the topic of conversation. When Stewart came into the mess another argument was raging.

"Your turn for hot showers to-morrow morning, chaps."

"What did Mueller want?" Peter asked.

"I don't know," Stewart said. "Just looking round, I think."

"D'you think he suspected anything?"

"Oh, I don't think so. Just came along to see what we were doing, I expect."

N

CHAPTER VI

SUDDENLY IT was spring. It seemed to Peter, as he walked from the barrack block to the White House for his shower, that the last few months had passed without his knowing it. He had been working hard on the tunnel, making his civilian clothes, planning a route; living in the future so intensely that he had not noticed the winter passing into spring. Now there was a hint of warmth in the air, even at this early hour, and outside the barrack blocks prisoners were shaking their bedding and flinging it over the clothes-lines which bordered the paths between the buildings. The sky was blue, and even the dark earth which not long since had been mud seemed to be expanding, stretching itself in the friendly sun. The air was strangely scented, and the warm sun on his face and hands quickened his blood, making him feel that life was good.

As he walked he decided that in future he would join Hugo in his cold shower before breakfast. It would be a discipline, something to get him fit for the trip that lay ahead. He would walk too, increasing distances round the circuit; two miles the first few days, then four, then six, up to twenty miles a day. He would not fail because he couldn't stay the distance. He would start to-morrow; for the moment he would make the most of the monthly hot shower, and change into the clean clothes that he carried under his arm.

" I paid sixpence to see
A tattooed Scotch lady,
She was a sight to see
Tattooed from head to knee———"

The words came through steam, the accompaniment was falling water, the tune *My Home In Tennessee*. Beneath a battery of twelve showers controlled by a German guard the prisoners unfolded like seedlings under a gardener's hose.

> " *Under her jaw*
> *Was the Royal Flying Corps*
> *And on her back*
> *Was the Union Jack,*
> *What could you ask for more?*
> *Up and down her spine*
> *Were the King's Own Guards in line*
> *And right around her hips*
> *Was a fleet of battleships——*"

Peter, lean and hard from hours of sweating in the tunnel, soaped himself all over and sang with the others.

> " *Over her kidney*
> *Was a bird's eye view of Sydney*
> *But what I liked best*
> *Upon her chest*
> *Was my home in Tennessee!*"

He was no longer just wasting his time, he had an objective now. Beside him John was singing in a high clear tenor.

Someone, a deep bass at the back of the room, began to sing *Wir Fahren Gegen England*. It was a good song to sing in the bath, and this was a typical bathroom. Their voices boomed and reverberated, aping the German Labour Corps who, in white cotton trousers, naked and bronzed above the waist and carrying burnished spades instead of rifles, marched past the camp in the mornings; marching on England by way of a road they were building through the forest.

> "*. . . England, England . . .*"

Then, high above the noise of the singers, Peter heard the shrill expostulation of the guard. "*Bitte, bitte!*" he was saying. The prisoners took no notice. Peter saw the guard's entreaties turn to fear, fear of the approach of a superior.

The fear turned to anger. He began to shout, as the Germans always shouted when they were nervous. The prisoners still ignored him. In desperation he turned off the water. It stopped suddenly, a few last miserable trickles mocking the soap-covered prisoners, who stared impotently at the guard. Slowly the singing subsided as, one by one, they admitted defeat. It was uncomfortable standing there in the cold, covered in nothing but wet soap. One or two of the more obstinate continued for a few bars, until the last was finally silenced by his comrades.

"*So!*" The *Obergefreiter* smiled, a smile of triumph. He turned the water on again.

"*I paid sixpence to see*
A tattooed Scotch lady . . ."

On their way back to the barrack block they noticed a crowd of prisoners gathering round the main gate. "What's going on down there?" John said.

"God knows—let's go and have a look."

As they walked down they met other prisoners converging from all directions, making towards the gate.

"What is it?" John asked one of them.

"New purge from *Dulag.*"

"Come on," Peter said, "there might be someone we know."

He hurried down to the gate, trying to curb his impatience, telling himself that his brother was not, could not, be there. Ever since his mother had written to tell him that Roy had been posted "missing" he had tried to stop himself from hoping that he would, one day, walk into the prison camp. To hope unreasonably, he felt, was a weakness. Nevertheless he knew the old choking sensation as he forced himself to walk more slowly as he neared the gate, could not prevent himself from almost running the last few yards.

Down at the gate the new purge was still standing in ranks outside the wire; pale, unshaven, bewildered men, most of them wearing the stiff new uniforms drawn from the stores at *Dulag-Luft*. Among them were some Americans, and these wore strange bulky flying boots and khaki jockey caps. They all looked tired, and there was an expression of horror on their faces as they regarded the uncouth bearded figures behind the wire. The kriegies were throwing over packets of cigarettes and calling out the numbers of their squadrons.

"Anyone from Seventy-five Squadron?"

"Yes—here!"

"How's old Tangletits?"

"Never heard of him."

Peter looked along the ranks of strange faces, looking for the mop of black hair, the upright, slim, disdainful figure; quickly at first, and then again more slowly. All around him other prisoners were crowding against the trip wire, only kept from the main fence by the machine-guns of the guards in the sentry boxes.

"Anyone from Seven Squadron?"

"Dick! God, I thought you'd fetch up here sooner or later! How's Jimmy?"

"Anyone from Coastal there?"

"Anyone from Thirty-five?"

Peter shouted the number of his squadron with the others and discovered a New Zealander who had been with the same squadron, but they did not know one another. He asked, casually, after his brother, but the man had never heard of him.

"Come and have tea with us this afternoon," Peter

suggested. "Block Four, the end mess. You can't miss it, it's next to the bog."

Then the gates were opened and the newcomers, hoisting their bundles on to their backs, straggled into the compound between the automatic rifles of their escort, who kept the older kriegies at a distance. As they passed the trip wire one of the Americans threw a small parcel which was caught by a kriegie. A guard, who had seen the parcel thrown, made a dart after it, but the kriegie quickly lost himself in the crowd. The American dodged unobtrusively behind his friends as they were marched up to the White House to be searched.

"Good show," Peter said. "That's something the goons won't get, anyway."

"Come on," John said, "we'll be late for lunch."

"I didn't see any Army chaps there," Peter said as they walked slowly away from the wire. He was ashamed that in his disappointment he had forgotten to introduce the New Zealander to John.

"There never are," John said.

"I've never understood how you came to be in an Air Force camp at all." Peter wanted to enter into John's life for a moment, to bury the insistent vision of his brother grimly holding his aircraft in that last screaming dive to the dark earth or sea below. "Why didn't they send you to an Army camp?"

"I was caught so far behind the German lines they thought I was a paratroop," John said. "Apparently they always send paratroops to Air Force camps."

"That's because their paratroops are part of the *Luftwaffe*," Peter told him. "What were you doing behind the German lines—sabotage?"

John grinned. "As a matter of fact—I wouldn't tell anyone else, mind—I was going in the wrong direction."

Peter laughed, glad of the excuse to laugh. He knew John well enough to be certain that he had not been captured

easily. He knew John's shame at having been captured, a
shame not shared by aircrew as their surrender had not
involved a laying down of arms. He changed the subject.
"You looked exactly as though you'd suddenly found
yourself in a zoo, that first day at *Dulag*. Absolutely lost.
It was being surrounded by the R.A.F., I expect."

"It was a bit disconcerting," John said, "but nothing to
the first day I came here. When I saw my first authentic
kriegies I swore that whatever happened I'd never let myself
get like that."

"And now look at us—I bet those new chaps are thinking
exactly the same about us."

"Some of us still keep pretty smart," John said. "Look
at Hugo—he shaves every morning and even polishes his
buttons with brickdust. I admire him for it, in a way.
It's a sort of self-respect."

"I don't think much of a self-respect that demands clean
buttons to keep it alive." The vision was fading now.
"That sort of thing's all right on the barrack square, but
it doesn't do much good out here. He's not adaptable, that's
all it is. He's the type that takes a dinner jacket on safari
with him."

"That's the type that built the Empire," John said.

"Don't you believe it, old son—not Hugo's type. The
Empire was built by jokers without backsides to their
trousers. You're thinking of the people who run it now."

"Better tell that to Loveday to-night in the mess," John
said.

"I'm not telling Loveday anything. I'm sick of arguments, we always seem to be arguing."

"We do argue a hell of a lot."

"Everyone does out here," Peter said. "I wonder what we
shall be like when we get back—it'll take some getting used
to. In some ways it's doing us good, I suppose . . . Y'know,
most of us have more freedom here than we've ever had in
our lives."

"That's good, too much freedom in a prison camp!"

"I mean it. Inside the fixed limits of the camp we're more free than we've ever been in our lives. If I decide I'll go and have tea with old Jones, and on the way there I meet Smith and decide to have tea with him instead, it doesn't matter. I've weeks and weeks to have tea with Jones in. If we want to stay in bed all day we can—look at Hugo again. After all, the essential freedom is freedom of mind —freedom from all businesses."

John laughed.

"Look at the way chaps are working here," Peter continued. "Enjoying hobbies and crafts they'd never have time for in normal life. Chaps painting and drawing who'd never have thought of it before they were captured. Studying too, and taking degrees. Chaps whose whole life up to now has been fully occupied in keeping alive. Now they're in the position of the idle rich as far as the arts are concerned. They don't have to worry about maintaining life, so they're free to enjoy it."

"But it's only a compensation," John said. "It sounds all right on the face of it, but after all it's only a compensation for what they're not allowed to have—the freedom of choice."

"The freedom to spend their whole lives in keeping alive?"

"Come off it, Pete. You know that need not be true of anyone these days."

"There's something in it anyway," Peter said. "It's lack of responsibility that gives the chaps time to develop their hobbies as they are doing."

"It's because they've nothing better to do," John said.

As they climbed the hill towards the barrack blocks they saw that their barrack was surrounded by small groups of prisoners who were being kept at a distance by armed guards. They began to hurry up the slippery path, wondering what had happened; Peter's private sorrow lessened now by the thought that something, anything, unusual was taking place.

They found Stewart arguing heatedly with Mueller in front of the door. "But it's lunchtime," Peter heard him say.

"I cannot help that, Mr. Stewart. If you will break the regulations by digging a tunnel from your barrack, you must expect to take the consequences."

"But this is mass punishment."

"Come, come, Mr. Stewart. You cannot call this mass punishment. It is merely a precaution."

There was a sudden crash as one of the small lockers, made by the prisoners from bed-boards, came hurtling out of an open window.

"You can hardly call that a precaution," Stewart said.

"You know perfectly well, Mr. Stewart, that it is against the regulations to make furniture out of the bed-boards."

From inside the block came the heavy bang, bang, of crowbars on the concrete floor, the rending crash as one of the lockers was pushed over on its side.

"Oh, go to hell!" Stewart said.

"There is no need to be violent, Mr. Stewart."

Peter and John stood among the other prisoners and watched their cherished possessions being hurled from the doors and windows to lie, sometimes broken, on the ground outside; mutilated books and photographs, carefully made shelves and cooking utensils, drawings and clothing, scattered or in heaps on the muddy ground.

"That's the end of the washhouse tunnel," John said. "Tyson said it wouldn't last for long."

"Mueller *was* after something the other night, then. I thought it was odd, coming round in the evening like that. Those damned dispersal bags of ours are still there, you know."

"They won't know what they are," John said.

"Of course they will, they've seen dispersal bags before."

He laughed. "They're under Saunders' bunk anyway—it'd do him good to have a spell in the cooler."

"It won't come to that," John said. "They'll just cart 'em away. We can easily make some more."

Towards the end of the afternoon Mueller called off the search. The washhouse tunnel had been found, so also had a number of *verboten* articles which were wrapped in blankets and taken away by the guards. The dispersal bags went with them. The tunnel, flooded with water for the night, would be filled in in the morning.

The end mess was in chaos. Mattresses had been ripped open, photographs torn from the walls, their small stocks of clean clothing lay scattered and trampled on the floor. "We'd better get cracking," Peter said. "We've got someone coming for tea."

"My pin-ups have gone!" Saunders shouted. "That bastard Mueller's pinched my pin-ups!"

Slowly they restored the room to some sort of order. Saunders, still devastated by the loss of the pin-up girls, grumbled as he worked, full of schemes to get even with Mueller.

The others took it in good spirit; only Loveday failed to respond. He sat on his bunk nursing *A Textbook of Psychology* which he had found with its back torn off among the debris on the floor. He did nothing towards clearing up the mess, but sat brooding, the book held listlessly between his hands.

"Come on, Loveday," Saunders said.

"Leave him," Otto said. "He will be all right in a minute." He began to sort out Loveday's things and put them away in his locker.

By the time the New Zealander arrived the room was more or less in order again. He hesitated in the doorway, as though afraid to enter.

"Come in," Peter said. "Excuse the chaos, we've just had a blitz." Then he remembered his own mystification on his first night in the prison camp. "The Germans found a tunnel in the washhouse," he explained.

"What are the chances of escape from here?" the New Zealander asked.

It had been one of Peter's own first questions, and he shelved it. Now that he was on a scheme himself he guarded it as jealously as the early gold prospectors had guarded their lucky strike. He felt that talking about it would minimise its value. Instead, he introduced the newcomer round the mess, but when he came to Loveday there was no response. The man seemed dead to the world. Peter passed it over as lightly as he could, and began to question the visitor about men he had known in the squadron. But he could find no point of contact. They had all been shot down, or posted to another squadron. Even the doctor and the padre had been changed.

When Hugo brought in the tea they sat down at the table.

Loveday remained obstinately on his bunk.

"Come on, Loveday—teatime!" Peter said. He put his hand on Loveday's shoulder, but there was no response. As he sat down he noticed the visitor glance as if fascinated at Loveday and then quickly look away.

We do look a queer lot I expect, he thought. He looked at the others; Saunders with his vulgar red good-humoured face, his impossible moustache, under his habitual knitted cap; Otto, pale and thin with woollen wrist-warmers showing below the cuffs of his tunic; John, a student from the Latin Quarter; Hugo, a stage Russian émigré, presiding at the head of the table; and Loveday sitting on his bunk like patience on a monument, brooding over the damage to his book.

He looked at the visitor and saw the hungry way in which he wolfed his bread and jam. His stomach will shrink, he thought, it'll take time, but in the end he won't be quite so hungry.

"Any good shows in Town?" Hugo made the opening gambit.

Peter saw the newcomer frantically searching his mind, and felt for him. "I don't suppose you had much time to go to shows," he suggested.

"No—used to spend most of the evenings with the boys."

"What's the beer like in England?" Saunders asked.

"It's all right. Pretty scarce."

"Ah," Saunders said. "It would be. How long've you been shot down?"

"Five days."

"Five days!" Saunders pushed his woollen cap to the back of his head. "Blimey, they aren't half pushing 'em through now. How long d'you have in the cooler?"

"The cooler?"

"Blimey," Saunders said, "he doesn't know he's alive." He examined their guest with renewed interest.

"How many trips had you done?" Hugo asked.

"This was my first trip."

Poor kid, Peter thought, what an end to your first trip. A year's training, one flight and now this. It was like the life of a butterfly. "You'll soon settle down," he said. "This isn't a bad life. It'll seem a little odd at first." What can I tell him about it, he thought, how can I advise him? "Have some more tea," he suggested.

"This is the end." Loveday's voice, deep and full of doom, coming from behind him, made the New Zealander choke into his mug.

"Hallo, Lovey." Saunders turned and looked at him. "Feeling better now the work's all done?"

"I've been meditating."

"Good thing," Saunders said. "Nothing like a little meditation when there's work to be done."

"They're frightened that I shall succeed now," Loveday said.

"Don't you worry, chum," Saunders told him. "Nothing you can't do if you put your mind to it."

"I *shall* succeed!" Loveday beat with his fist on the side of his bunk. "You individuals fail to realise how organised they are. They even try to destroy my work."

"You'll disorganise 'em." Saunders winked at the New Zealander. "Just keep on the way you're going."

Loveday came to the table and glared at them. "So we have strangers in the mess."

Otto poured him a cup of tea and passed his three slices of bread and butter, while Peter began to tell the New Zealander about the events of the afternoon. All the time he was talking he could see the boy stealing furtive glances at Loveday who, eating stolidly through his bread and butter, fixed him with a malevolent stare.

"Well, I'd better be getting on." The guest rose to his feet and moved towards the doorway. "Thanks very much for the tea."

"Not a bit," Peter said. "Come and see us again some time."

"I will." The New Zealander stole one more frightened glance at Loveday and escaped into the corridor.

CHAPTER VII

A S SPRING slowly relaxed into summer the two remaining tunnels were driven painfully inch by inch at right angles to one another towards the wire. The *abort dienst* was well in the lead, and for the past few weeks Tyson's team had worked desperately to catch them up. If they could make sufficient headway both tunnels could break on the same night, and a record number of prisoners would get away. If Stewart broke first, the second tunnel would be handicapped by the stringent security measures that would inevitably follow the first escape. It was a back-breaking race against time and, hampered by water seepage, the cookhouse team were unable to maintain the pace. By the middle of May the *abort* attempt was ready to break. The escapers had prepared their forged papers and their civilian clothes, and now they waited for a suitable night to make their getaway.

Tyson had decided to suspend work on the cookhouse tunnel until after the others had broken out. As he explained to his disappointed team, "We could hardly expect them to wait for us and it would be a pity if we made a boob now and gave the other show away. We can't possibly get ready to break on the same night so we'll just have to lie low until they've gone. As soon as the flap's lifted we can get cracking again."

Peter and John, stifling their impatience, used this period of idleness to perfect the plans for their own journey. They had decided to walk down through Poland and attempt to make contact with the partisan forces in Yugoslavia. They would travel as Italians and John, who already had a smattering of the language, was working hard at his Italian grammar. At the same time he was learning the part of Lysander for the new production of *A Midsummer Night's Dream*, which was to be staged in the early summer. Peter knew that he regarded this as an insurance against their tunnel being discovered.

On the day that the *abort* tunnel broke England played Australia at rugby football. Under cover of the enormous crowds Stewart's team, their escape clothing hidden by greatcoats, wandered down to the *abort* and, one by one, lowered themselves into the trench and so into the narrow tunnel. In addition to the digging team there were the dispersal squads, some stooges, and one or two of the prisoners who had helped to forge the identity papers or make the civilian clothes. Some of these had never been down the tunnel before and there were long delays while they rearranged their packs and clothing before they could squeeze into the narrow hole. At last there were more than thirty of them, lying head to heels along the suffocating length of the muddy burrow.

Peter had given up football now that his own escape seemed possible. To risk a broken leg at this stage would be foolish. He helped Tyson to get the last man down a few minutes before lock-up time, and went back to the barrack block. Most of the thirty escapers had come from Block 2, but the vacant spaces had been evenly distributed over the entire camp. Several people had gone to spend the night in another block, and in the empty bunks cleverly made dummies lay under the grey blankets, wigs made from human hair and empty boots protruding naturally.

It was a perfect night for escape. Heavy clouds were massing in an angry sky. Gusts of wind went humming through the wire, blowing into the camp, and causing the guards to turn their backs to its source—turn their backs on the potato patch which lay in the path of the bitter wind, and which intricate calculations with line and home-made theodolite had told the tunnellers would cover the exit of their tunnel.

Under the potato patch the working party dug away the last few feet of subsoil and waited for complete darkness.

In Peter's block all the preparations had been made. Following the discovery of the escape, there would be a search such as they had never had before; a search that would sweep in its ruthless path everything that was in the least suspect. During that afternoon most of them had buried everything of value in the ground outside the barrack. Peter and John had buried their home-made civilian clothes and their store of carefully hoarded food; but Peter could not bear to part with his small brass compass and the maps he had brought with him from *Dulag-Luft*. He had sewn these into the waistband of his trousers.

Now he sat with the others who, trying to appear as usual, were all the time half-listening for the sudden rifle shot or the angry stutter of machine-guns which would tell them that the escapers had been seen by the guards outside the wire.

"Dinner's an hour early to-night," Saunders warned them.

"Good show," Peter said.

"They've made them all an hour earlier in case . . . you know," Saunders said.

"What are we having?" John asked.

"Salmon pie."

"Not again!"

"Well . . . I can do it quickly, you see—in case anything happens. By the way"—defensively—"there's no chocolate this week."

"How's that?" Hugo liked his chocolate.

"I gave it to Otto."

"Oh, you did, did you?"

"Well—I didn't really *give* it to him. After all, we've got the rest of his parcel this week."

"Yes, that's right."

"I gave him the raisins too," Saunders said. He seemed to expect censure for this.

"That's O.K.," Peter said. "You're the cook. As long as you dish us up a meal each day——"

"There's no sweet," Saunders said quickly. "I gave him the sugar too."

Loveday kept to his bunk all evening, speaking to no one, refusing to be drawn into conversation. He had been like this ever since Otto had told him that he was leaving. He had told him alone, out on the circuit, and the others did not know how Loveday had taken it. They only knew that this strange silence, instead of being a blessing, was a curse. His brooding cast a blight upon them all, and they were unable to settle down.

The whole barrack block was quiet, everyone listening with half his mind for the sound of a shot and the whistles of the guards. Everyone, with half his mind, was crawling out through the muddy exit through the rows of growing potatoes, away from the camp. Everyone shared the feeling of naked vulnerability, the "crab-without-shell" feeling of the man with a gun behind him; the feeling they had all known at least once before, when their aircraft had heeled and spiralled down in flame.

"What about a game of cards?" Saunders' suggestion was tentative.

"Not to-night," Hugo said.

"Where's Otto making for?" Saunders asked.

"Warsaw," Peter told him.

"Rum sort of place to make for."

"He was born there."

"Oh, yes, of course—he's a Pole."

There was a silence. Someone in a mess at the far end of the room started the gramophone. They sat listening to it; the first time they had ever listened to it consciously, as anything other than a background to their conversation.

"Damn' stupid lyric," Peter said.

"All dance lyrics are stupid," Hugo said.

"Why don't you finish that story of yours, Saunders?" Peter asked.

"If the lights go out. It's a bedtime story, only to be told in the dark." Half-heartedly Saunders picked up a paintbrush he was making for Peter; rolling sisal string into a hank, cutting the loops with a razor blade, fraying them out and binding the rest to form a handle.

"A bedroom story, you mean," Hugo said.

"I wonder if they're all out yet?" John looked up from his book.

Peter glanced at his watch. "Not yet. There are thirty of them. If you allow an interval of three minutes between each, it's going to take an hour and a half. Better allow another hour for safety. If we hear nothing by nine o'clock we can reckon they're all away."

"Another hour and a half," Saunders said.

"It's going to be a hell of a day to-morrow." Hugo was darning a sock, using a tin of baked beans as a mushroom. "What are you doing about your job?"

"Leave it alone for at least another week," Peter told him. "Wouldn't be safe to go near it before then. The goons will tighten up like hell for a bit after this."

"That's the worst of tunnels," Hugo said. "Everybody suffers. It isn't only you chaps."

"Every tunnel that breaks means one less starting place," John said.

"It must have been wonderful for the chaps who were the first ones here," Peter said. "Fancy being in a camp from which no one had ever started a tunnel . . ."

"It would be very pleasant, I agree," Hugo said. "But sooner or later chaps would start digging and the goons would start imposing restrictions. It's a sort of vicious circle, one chasing the other. Far better not to start it."

"Far better not to be here at all," John said.

"It makes you think." Saunders sat hunched over the table, wearing the woollen cap that seemed so much part of his face, the paintbrush forgotten in his struggle to express himself. "It makes you realise that no man has any right to lock a fellow up for any length of time. Look at us. Compared to Dartmoor this place is a holiday camp. We've got our friends, and the goons leave us pretty well alone. Yet we think it's bloody awful here. Fancy going to Dartmoor for twenty or thirty years. A hundred and ninety-nine years they can give you in America. Rather get the chop."

"We don't know how long we've got," Hugo said.

"I'd rather not know," Peter said.

"I like to know where I am." Hugo bit off an end of wool and moved the tin round inside the sock, looking for more holes. "If we only knew how long we'd got, we'd know how long we had to wait."

"We're not doing so bad," Saunders said. "Think of those chaps in Dartmoor. For what? Because they stole to feed their wives and kids most likely. And why did they steal? Because no one had ever taught them how to earn their living."

"They broke the law, they must face the consequences," Hugo said. "Our case is different, we're not criminals."

"We all got caught," John said.

"We're just as guilty as they are, if it comes to that," Saunders said. "Look at me—I've killed thousands of innocent women and children, bombed hospitals and churches——"

"The Bermondsey Basher, they call him," John said. "Slit-throat Saunders."

"No, but a man who commits bigamy gets seven years in the cooler." Saunders was not to be sidetracked. "Not seven years of this, but in a grey cell, never seeing grass or trees. And for what? Just because he married two women at the same time, and probably made 'em both happy. And did it honourably too. After all, he could have married one and slept with the other, and no one would have had any objection."

"Except his wife, perhaps," John said.

"But if you make laws you must enforce them," Hugo said. "What would happen if there were no punishment for crime—the country would be in chaos."

"Yes, but seven years!" Saunders rose to his feet and crossed to his bunk for a cigarette. "Some of us think our lives are ruined, and we've only been here two or three. Think of a life sentence—think of it! We've only one life, it's the only one we've got, and some old beak in a white wig can make us spend it all in prison. It's far more humane to shoot people out of hand."

"Well, how would you punish a bigamist if you didn't send him to prison?" Hugo asked. "Shoot him?"

"Well, the only people he's done any harm to are the two women." Saunders was obviously thinking this out. "If the first one still wants him, I'd scrap the second marriage, and let 'im fight it out with the first." He blew out a cloud of smoke and watched it swirl under the naked electric lamp. "If the second one wants him and the first doesn't, scrap the first marriage. If they both want him, the first one wins. If neither want him, you scrap both marriages," he finished triumphantly.

"It wouldn't work," Hugo said. "Besides, you've got the wrong end of the stick. We don't send him to prison for living with two women. We send him to prison for false pretences. As you say, he can live with as many women as he likes—as long as he doesn't marry them. Marriage is a contract, and you must protect both parties to it."

"The best way to do that would be to have it stamped on your identity card," Saunders said. "You'd produce your twelve-fifty when you want to get married, and prove you're not married already. It would be impossible to commit bigamy then."

"Bureaucracy!" Hugo said, starting on another sock. "Bigamy is a felony, and it's up to the State to prove that you've committed it, not up to you to prove that you're not about to commit it. It works pretty well as it is."

"Yes—but seven years!" Saunders said. "Fancy some skinny old beak having the power to lock a chap up for seven years, just because he's made a mistake. I reckon all judges ought to go to prison for a year, as part of their training—just to show 'em what it's like. We've almost abolished flogging, and we ought to do the same with long-term sentences. What's the use of it? It's horrible. It doesn't do the prisoner any good, it's just done as a warning to others, like cutting off their hands and noses used to be. It's time it was stopped."

"That's right, Saunders," John said. "Let's start a prison reform."

"I mean it," Saunders said. "I'd never thought about it before. Now I wonder how people can walk about the streets knowing that behind those walls there are hundreds of people locked up for years."

"It's better than having them loose," Hugo said.

They sat in silence, in the strangely silent room. The gramophone was still playing, but quietly now, in a mess at the far end of the room; and Peter imagined the sentries stamping up and down outside the wire, swinging their arms to keep warm, fleetingly illuminated by the passing searchlight beams.

"What about that story?" Hugo said.

"I'm not in the mood." Saunders was unusually serious to-night.

"Come on—we've got to do something to pass the time."

John took a tattered piece of paper from his pocket. "I'll read you a poem if you like. That'll cheer you up." He straightened the paper and announced:

"Night Bombers

"*Monstrous shadows moving in the darkness*
In sudden bursts of power in near-dawn darkness;
Huge ungainly lumbering shapes
Wallowing blindly towards dispersal points,
Waved onwards and finally brought to rest
By two dim lights
Wielded commandingly by an airman,
Cold in the exterior darkness.

"*From the belly of the nearest shadow*
Descends a ladder, down which climb
Seven leather-huge dwarf men.
Michelin-men of uncouth shape;
Helmeted and visored like men from Mars
And, as they stiffly clamber down,
The wind blows freshly; brings the friendly smell
Of earth and meadows in the moonlight.

"*For nine hours these have been away from earth,*
Sucking oxygen through narrow tubes,
Cold and cramped and deaf with noise,
Each in his lonely station;
While searchlights, flak and fighters all combine
To tear them down;
To tear them fiercely burning from the sky,
In which they try in vain to hide themselves.

"*So slowly down they clamber,*
Remove their masks and sniff the air;
They light a cigarette and stretch their arms
And look around them at the sky.
They are glad to be alive these men;
These seven leather-huge dwarf men
As thick-booted gloved and helmeted they stand
Beneath the belly of that monstrous bird."

"That's not a poem," Saunders said. "It doesn't rhyme."

"You didn't write it, did you?" Peter spoke to John.

"No."

"Who did?"

"I don't know. I found it when we were putting the dummies in the bunks."

"If you want some poetry," Saunders said, "I know a bit of *Gunga Din*."

"I wonder who wrote it," Peter said.

"Kipling, of course!" Saunders said it with scorn.

"No—I mean this. Let's have a look, John." He took the paper from John's hand. "Why, this is Otto's writing."

"Blimey," Saunders said. "I didn't know Otto was a poet. He couldn't speak English, hardly."

"His English was good," John said. "It was only his accent that was a bit ropey."

"That happens to be my property," Loveday said, from his bunk, "and I'll thank you to give it to me."

"Sorry." Peter passed the piece of paper to Loveday who took it, folded it and put it under his pillow.

"I think it's jolly good." Peter would have said more, have tried to tell Loveday that they understood, that they realised that this evening meant more to him than it did to them. But it had grown beyond that. Loveday had put himself beyond their reach.

"Come on, Saunders, let's have that story." Hugo beckoned them away from Loveday's bunk.

"O.K. Where was I?"

"In Montreal," John said. "You'd just met the old dame, and she'd shown you into a room on the left of the hall."

"No—it was on the right of the hall, just as you came in through the door."

"O.K., it was the right. What happened then?"

"I told you about the drawings, didn't I?"

"Yes—you didn't describe them."

"God, what drawings they were! It'd shake old Mueller

if I had 'em here. All in colour they were. Makes we sweat to think of them. And the whole place smelled of bath salts, a sort of choky, expensive smell. We sat on one of the seats and the old girl said, ' The girls won't be a moment,' and waddled off down the hall. We thought she meant the waitresses."

"Come off it," Hugo said.

"Honestly! We both thought we were going to get our tea. I asked old Dicky about it afterwards, and he still thought we were getting our tea."

"Then what happened?"

"Well, we sat there for a bit, then I got up and walked around, looking at the drawings. Jolly good they were, too. Then I heard footsteps and darted back and sat down next to Dicky. Then the old dame came in followed by a lot of girls, and we realised that it wasn't a tea-shop after all." He stopped abruptly.

"Go on," Hugo said.

"Give it a rest to-night," Saunders said. "I told you, I'm not in the mood. I can't keep on talking while that goes on outside. Let's play cards or something."

"It must be about our turn for the stove," Hugo said. "Come on."

While Hugo and Saunders were preparing dinner Peter sat and listened for the sound of activity from outside, but heard nothing.

He went to the latrine whose window looked out on to the wire, and found Tyson there, gazing intently out into the darkness.

"Anything happening?" Peter asked.

"They must be all away by now," Tyson said. "I'd give my ears to be with them."

"We'll be out soon," Peter said.

"It's too much to hope for, two tunnels so close together," Tyson said. "We'll be lucky if we survive the search."

When Peter got back to the mess the others were sitting

round the table, eating and discussing poetry. "Come on, Pete," John said, "yours is getting cold."

"I can never understand how people can remember poetry," Hugo was saying. "There was a chap at school who knew the whole of *Paradise Lost* by heart."

"It's perfectly easy," John said. "Merely a matter of application. This pie's jolly good, Hugo."

"It's not overcooked," Hugo said. "The secret is a slow but constant heat."

"My God, you make me sick!" Loveday shouted. "Talk—talk—talk! Why can't some of you keep quiet for a change!"

"Listen to who's talking now," Saunders said.

"Give it a rest to-night, Saunders," Hugo said.

"It must need a peculiar sort of brain to remember poetry," Peter said. "I once knew a fellow who could do an extraordinary thing. If you gave him a list of thirty perfectly unconnected words and allowed him to look at it for five minutes, he could put the list away and repeat it from memory—from top to bottom and from bottom to top. Then he could start from number fifteen and repeat them backwards to number one, go back to number sixteen and repeat down to number thirty."

"It must be a very peculiar sort of brain," Saunders said.

"I reckon I could do it," John said.

"Don't talk cock!" Loveday exploded all his pent-up personal animosity, all his rage and fear, in the single sentence.

"I said that I reckon I could do it."

"Bet you two bars of chocolate you can't." Loveday glared at him in challenge.

The mess was silent. Two bars of chocolate was a big stake.

Two bars of chocolate represented a fortune. Peter and John had been saving their chocolate for weeks now; refusing to eat it, hiding it in the back of their locker and going to look at it now and again—just to see that it was still there—but keeping it for the escape, hoarding it with a few dried raisins and the odd Horlicks tablet they had begged from the British doctor in the camp hospital. Now it was hidden outside with the rest of their kit. Loveday, apparently, did not set so much store by chocolate.

"I'll take you on," John said.

"Well, don't do it until after I've cleared the dinner things away," Hugo told him. "This is going to be interesting."

"I must have complete quiet," John said.

"Right," Peter said. "Now, quiet, chaps—it's only for five minutes."

John sat with his elbows on the table, head between his hands, gazing at the piece of paper on which Hugo had printed the list of words. The others watched; Peter and Hugo at each end of the table, Saunders and Loveday from their bunks. John folded the paper, and handed it to Peter. Slowly he began:

"Smoke . . .
milk . . .
rafters . . .
window . . .
anticipation . . .
rogue . . .
paper . . .
bathe . . .
clog . . .
onomatopœia . . .
meat-roll . . ."

He paused for a moment.

"Cliff . . .
steeplechase . . .
rapids . . .
stooge . . .
rationalise . . .

lipstick . . .
chesterfield . . .
baggage . . .
clay . . .
beefsteak . . .
pipe . . .
sanitation . . ."
He paused again, for longer this time, while Peter willed
him to remember.
"Jargon . . .
Chanel Five . . .
eggs . . .
theatre . . .
goon . . .
table . . .
triumph."
"Good show!" Peter said. "Now from bottom to top."
John sat with his head in his hands and repeated very
slowly, "Triumph, table . . ." all the way through to
"cliff."
"Very good indeed," Peter said. "Now from 'stooge' to
the top."
"Give 'im the chocolate!" Saunders said.
"No," Peter said, "he can do it." He wanted them to win
it fairly.
John held up his hand for silence. Slowly and deliberately
he repeated the first fifteen backwards, then from sixteen
to thirty.
"I'd never have believed it possible," Peter said.
"There's nothing outstanding in that," Loveday said.
"Visual memory, that's all."
"It's cost you two bars of chocolate anyway," Saunders
told him.
"That's as may be."
"What d'you mean?"
"How do you know Howard wasn't prompting?"

"Because I was watching. So were you for that matter."

"I'm not convinced."

"What more proof d'you want?" Peter said. "You saw him do it. Come on, give him the chocolate."

"I haven't got two bars of chocolate anyway."

"Well!" Saunders said. "You bastard!"

Loveday jumped to his feet, but stood transfixed. A queer rasping cry broke from his lips. The others watched him, appalled. Slowly a tremor ran through his body, his face began to twitch. There was a fixed, murderous, yet frightened look in his eyes. He took one step towards Saunders, who, also frightened, began to rise from his bunk; then Loveday crashed to the ground, panting for breath and blubbering, his lips flecked with reddish foam.

"Get him on to the bed," Peter said. He took out his handkerchief and tried to force it between Loveday's teeth, but they were tightly clenched.

"Get the M.O.," Hugo said.

"We can't—the doors are locked."

"Get Stewart."

"Don't be a bloody fool," Saunders said. He giggled nervously. "He's half-way across Poland by now."

"It's all right," Peter said. "He'll be all right." He covered Loveday with a blanket, and loosened the collar round his neck.

"What the hell's wrong with him?" Saunders asked.

"Epileptic fit," Peter said.

"D'you think I caused it?"

"You shouldn't have called him a bastard," Hugo said. "Some people can't stand that."

"Some people are bastards." Saunders was recovering.

Slowly Loveday's breathing grew more normal, till he seemed merely to be sleeping.

"Leave him now," Peter said. "When he wakes he'll have forgotten all about it."

"He scared the pants off me," Saunders said.

They sat in silence for a while listening to Loveday's heavy breathing.

"We ought to get him put in the hospital," Peter said.

"They wouldn't accept him," John said. "He's perfectly normal for most of the time."

"I wouldn't go so far as that," Saunders said.

That night Peter could not sleep. He lay on his bunk wondering about the escapers, where they were and what they were doing. He imagined those who had decided to go on foot walking along the deserted roads of the Polish countryside; free. Free to go wherever they liked. And now, if the cookhouse tunnel weathered the search and was not discovered, they could start on theirs again. He and John were well up on the list. The bad air and the damp of the tunnel had already taken its toll of the diggers. One by one they had dropped out, and place by place he and John had crept towards the top. Now they were well within the coveted "first ten" and would be certain of getting away when the tunnel broke.

He would soon have to arrange for the rest of his civilian clothes and his papers; he wouldn't worry about these until after the search. Too bad to get all ready and then lose the lot. Far better not to make too many preparations—too much to lose if you were discovered.

In the early morning, still unable to sleep, he went out to the washhouse for a mug of water. The place was lit by a feeble low-powered bulb, and beneath the light Tyson, muffled in coats and blankets, sat reading a book. He did not look up as Peter entered the room, nor did he speak. As Peter filled his mug quietly, anxious not to disturb him, Tyson slowly turned a page, and when he left the washhouse the man was still sitting there, his head bent to the book in the dim light, alone in the night-quiet washhouse.

CHAPTER VIII

THE FOLLOWING morning the usual body of miserable green-clad German soldiers with fixed bayonets marched into the compound, separated to the various barrack blocks, unlocked the doors and shouted their usual "'*Raus, 'raus!*'" to call the prisoners to another day. In Peter's block the prisoners shouted back their usual reply.

But here ended the similarity to any other morning. Instead of breakfast of three thin slices of black bread, Saunders and Hugo had prepared a substantial meal—not as a celebration, but because very soon the whole camp would be turned out on to the football pitch to stand, perhaps all day, while the tunnel was excavated and the barracks searched.

This morning, to make the columns look their normal length, the prisoners paraded in ranks of three instead of five. They were all fully dressed and carried sandwiches, some of them cardboard boxes full of food. No one knew what to expect, and it was wise to be prepared.

To Hauptmann Mueller as he walked up the hill, everything looked as it normally did. There were the long lines of prisoners, each line nearly as long as the barrack before which it stood. Peter's block was the first to be counted, Wing-Commander Stewart's place being taken by Tyson, who in unaccustomed full uniform looked tired and apprehensive.

As Mueller approached, Tyson saluted. The German returned his salute.

"Where is Mr. Stewart?"

"He is not here this morning."

"*Ach so?*" Mueller looked slowly down the ranks of grinning men. It was not until the guards began the count that he became aware that everything was not in order. His round face turned white, then red, then white again. Peter could see the effort that he was exerting to retain control.

He turned to Tyson. "In fives, please," he said in a quiet voice. "Always in fives, Mr. Tyson."

"O.K., chaps—close up!"

Untidily the long straggling line of prisoners closed up to a compact bunch three-quarters of its normal length. Mueller, determined not to betray his feelings, stood silent while the count was taken. There were fifteen prisoners missing.

He moved to the next block, where the same performance was repeated. He counted all the blocks, and then stood talking to the *Lagerfeldwebel* in the middle of the square. By now the triumphant prisoners could see from his face that he was beside himself with worry. Presently the *Feldwebel* called one of the guards, who saluted and set off at the double to the *Kommandantur*.

The prisoners waited expectantly. Then the rumour got around that Mueller had sent for the *Kommandant*. He was an almost mythical being, rarely seen in the compound. Mueller walked up and down, his hands behind his back, while the *Feldwebel* loosened stones from the path with the toes of his jackboot and kicked them against the wall of the barrack block.

Presently the compound gates were opened, and a squad of guards, armed with tommy-guns and wearing steel helmets, marched towards the football pitch. They were halted and turned to face the prisoners, their tommy-guns at the ready.

"Mass execution at *Oflag XXIB*," John muttered.

"They're only closing the stable door," Peter assured him. In spite of the danger to their tunnel, he was enjoying himself, as most of the prisoners were enjoying this break in the normal routine.

There was a murmur of appreciation as the *Kommandant*, a slight figure in cavalry breeches and a long flowing cloak, appeared at the gates. He walked stiffly, like an ancient crow, his cloak held tightly across his narrow chest. *Hauptmann* Mueller walked down to meet him, the roll fluttering in his hand. They met, watched by nine hundred prisoners. The *Lageroffizier* saluted and stood stiffly to attention while the *Kommandant*, having returned the salute, stood arms akimbo, his cloak blowing in the wind.

"He's tearing old Mueller off a terrific strip," John said.

"Wouldn't be in his shoes," Saunders said. "Not for six months off my sentence." He chuckled nervously.

The two Germans talked for some minutes while the troops drawn up on the football pitch stood stiffly, pointing their tommy-guns at the prisoners. Then Mueller saluted again, turned on his heel, and walked back towards the barrack blocks. When he reached the top of the hill his face was set in a frozen grin; the British prisoners must see that he was "sporting."

"You will return to your quarters, gentlemen," he said.

The prisoners filed back into their barrack blocks, and were locked in.

The rumour spread quickly; the *Kommandant* had sent to Berlin for the *Gestapo*. In Peter's block there were long queues for the windows that looked out on to the football pitch. The fortunate ones who had obtained the point of vantage were relaying the news to those inside the room.

"Here come some more goons."

"They must have turned out the whole unit," another said. "There are hundreds of goons marching down the road."

"They've deployed into the fields now—they're surrounding the camp. They're making a loose cordon about fifty yards deep."

"They've no idea where the tunnel comes out, that's why."

"They've no idea where it starts either."

There was a silence, while those at the back grew restless.

"What's happening now?"

"Nothing much—they're just hanging around looking stupid."

"Here come the dogs."

"Where—I can't see them!"

"There, look—coming along the road behind the sentry-box."

"Hell, yes—it won't be long now, chaps."

"Here comes a car. Two cars—three—a whole convoy. They're Mercs, they're stopping outside the gates. Brown uniform—must be the *Gestapo*. They're all saluting one another now. Heiling Hitler as hard as they can go."

"What are the dogs doing?"

"They're quartering the fields outside the wire. They've found the tunnel!"—excitedly—"they're hopping about like mad—they're shouting their heads off at one another. How typical, how bloody typical! Someone's run off for the *Kommandant*. He's fallen over his rifle. What clots—they're pointing their rifles down the hole—as though anyone's still down there!"—shouting out of the window—"You clots, you damned silly clots! They went hours ago!"

"Shut up, Bill," someone said. "They'll put a bullet in here if you don't shut up."

"Sorry, but they *are* silly clots. Look at them standing there as though they expect the whole camp to come out of the hole."

"Here comes the *Kommandant*. And the Wily Gest-a-po. And the cameramen. They look as though they're going to a funeral."

"Have you fellows had enough yet? Let someone else have a look."

The window party squeezed their way out, those immediately behind taking their places.

P

"What's happening now?"

"They've got to the hole. They're all waving their arms about. I can't see what they're doing, I think the *Kommandant* is telling old Mueller to go down the hole. He's refusing to go."

"Mueller's telling one of the goons to go down—he's refusing to go too."

"Good show, that's mutiny. Hope they shoot the whole bloody lot."

"What are they doing now?"—impatiently.

"One of them's got a bicycle—he's cycling back to the compound."

"The *Kommandant's* lighting a cigarette. They're taking a photograph of the hole. Fat lot of good that's going to be."

"That's for the records, old boy. The Scene Of The Amazing Break At *Oflag XXIB*. Thirty Desperadoes Loose in Poland. The *Luft-Gangsters'* Break For Freedom."

"Hallo, there's a squad of goons coming into the compound. They're marching across to the *abort*. They must know the tunnel starts from there."

"Left right, left right, left right . . ." the prisoners chanted in time with the marching soldiers. Slowly they changed the time of their shouting, and burst into laughter as the Germans altered step. It's just like school, Peter thought. He stood at the back of the crowd listening to the running commentary. He felt the victory of the prisoners over their guards and, as always in moments of victory, he felt pity for the vanquished.

"Left right, left right . . ." There was the sudden rattle of a stick brushed across corrugated iron as a salvo of tommy-gun fire flew low across the roof of the barrack block.

"Better pack it in, chaps," someone said. "The next lot'll be through the windows."

"What's happening now?"

"They've locked the door of the *abort*, and posted a couple of goons outside."

"Perhaps now they've found the tunnel they'll let us out of here."

"Not a hope, we'll be here for days."

"I bet they don't find the trap from this end. We sealed it down pretty thoroughly."

"Here come the working party. They've got some Ruskis with spades. They're going to make 'em dig it up."

"Where from? The *abort* end?"

"No—the exit. They're telling a Ruski to go down— they're putting a Ruski down the hole. Poor devil, he'll come out right into the trench of the *abort*."

"He's lucky—they'll have to give him a bath now."

"He'll never get through it. I expect half the chaps left their food down there because they couldn't carry it all."

"Old Kee went out loaded like a camel."

There was silence as the green-clad Russian prisoner was seen to crawl headfirst into the tunnel. Presently there was more excitement.

"Look—here come some charabancs. They're pulling up outside the camp. They're full of goons—hundreds of 'em —complete with kit and everything."

Saunders came and joined Peter and Loveday at the back of the crowd. "They haven't got a chance," he said.

"There are too many of them," Peter said. "If only one or two had gone they wouldn't have taken all this trouble. Thirty going all at once has scared them stiff. They're turning half the army out."

"It's going to make it difficult for your lot when you break," Saunders said.

"They'll forget all about it before then," Peter told him.

"I hope Otto gets away," Saunders said. "I reckon he's got more chance than the others."

"More chance of getting shot if he's caught." Peter saw the look on Loveday's face and wished that he had not spoken.

The prisoners were locked in the barrack blocks all that day and night, and the following morning the whole camp was herded on to the football pitch, where they were surrounded by a ring of armed guards while the buildings were searched. They spent the morning sitting and standing —there was not room for them all to sit at the same time —or queuing to use the temporary latrine that had been erected in one corner of the pitch. Saunders had brought his patent portable *Stufa* and Peter and the few prisoners who surrounded them were able to drink a mug of luke-warm tea.

Later in the morning the Germans set up a trestle-table under one of the goalposts. One by one the prisoners were made to approach the table, where they were identified with the complete personal record kept by the Germans—photograph, fingerprints, birthmarks and a chart of tooth fillings. After each man had been identified he was stripped and searched; and then he was released to walk freely round the circuit, but was not allowed to enter the barrack blocks.

The prisoners quickly realised that the longer they could spin out this identity parade, the greater start would the escapers have. They milled around inside the cordon of guards, each one, as he was caught and taken to the table, hanging back like a frightened steer about to be branded. Once he was in front of the table deliberate misunderstanding and stupidity, if handled intelligently, could gain a valuable ten minutes. After half an hour of this the guards used their bayonets to enforce their commands, and the identification was speeded up.

As the football pitch thinned out and Peter realised that it would soon be his turn to be identified, he began to worry about the few *verboten* possessions that were hidden in his clothes. There would be a serious shortage of maps and compasses for the next few weeks and he did not want to go out unprepared. In spite of Tyson's pessimism he was still confident that their tunnel would remain undiscovered. Surely the goons would be content with one tunnel unearthed this week.

Looking round him to see what the others were doing, he could see several earnest bearded figures diligently but furtively scraping away with their hands at the loose earth of the football pitch, or patting the surface soil tenderly back into place. He knew a moment's indecision and then quickly slid his maps and compass from their hiding-place in the waistband of his trousers and buried them in the ground. Shortly afterwards he was taken by the guards and marched to the trestle-table where Mueller, a chastened man, sat glowering through his round, dark-rimmed spectacles.

"Number?"

"Eh?"

"Number?"

"Number?"

Mueller kept his temper. "Your P.O.W. identity number!"

"Oh . . . I've forgotten it."

"Where is your disc?"

"Disc?"

Mueller signalled to one of the guards, who lowered his rifle and gently pushed the bayonet into the small of Peter's back.

"Oh, my *disc*!" Peter fumbled with the front of his shirt, taking as long as he could to discover the metal disc which hung from a piece of string round his neck. When, at last, he found it, the string was too short to enable him to read the number. He leaned across the table and held the disc in front of the officer's face.

Mueller drew back hastily. "*So! Neunundachtzig!*" He flicked through a small box file and extracted a card, in one corner of which Peter could see a photograph of himself with set expression, holding a number across his chest.

"Flight-Lieutenant Peter Howard." Mueller studied the photograph, then looked hard at Peter. "So you have been in bad company. Do not congratulate yourself, my friend. They will not be out for long." He signalled the guard to take him along to be searched.

At last, when all the prisoners had been identified and released on to the circuit, a close line of guards walked methodically across the football pitch, turning over the loose soil with their jackboots. Peter, standing by the touchline, watched anxiously as penknives, compasses, maps, indian ink, packets of dye and other escape material were unearthed and placed in two large blankets which the ferrets carried off to the *Kommandantur*.

As soon as the prisoners were allowed on the pitch he went to where he buried his things; but the compass and maps had gone.

During the next ten days the prisoners were awakened five or six times every night to be counted, land-mines were placed in the earth outside the wire, and series of snap *appels* were held. These were carried out independently of the usual fixed roll-calls and were heralded by the blowing of a bugle. As soon as the bugle sounded the prisoners had to leave whatever they were doing and assemble outside the barrack blocks. While they were being counted ferrets searched the blocks, the *aborts*, the cookhouse and the wash-houses in the hope of finding a tunnel which the sudden roll-call had forced the prisoners to leave uncovered.

Under these conditions it was impossible to dig, and Tyson decided not to resume work on the cookhouse tunnel until this security mood of the guards had passed. Peter and John, chafing at the delay, passed the time in walking round the circuit to keep fit and in making their plans for the long journey across Poland and Hungary to Yugolsavia.

Gradually the excitement subsided and one by one, sometimes in pairs, the would-be escapers were brought back,
grinning sheepishly, into the fold. The cooler was already
filled with the victims of the *Kommandant's* displeasure on
the morning after the break, and the returned escapers were
locked in the White House where they lay awaiting trial.
Often on their daily walk round the circuit Peter and John
would catch a glimpse of the white strained faces peering
from the upper windows. A levy was made on all rations,
and food was sent to these prisoners within a prison.

Eventually only Otto and an English lieutenant-com-
mander were still at large. As the days grew into weeks
their fellow prisoners began to hope that these two had got
clean away. When at last the news came that they had been
"shot while resisting arrest," the camp refused to believe
what they hoped was merely a rumour. Then it was announced publicly on parade by the S.B.O. and the prisoners
were forced to accept it.

They retaliated by increasing their goon-baiting activities
until there was open warfare between the prisoners and their
guards. The Germans, frightened by this hatred, used their
rifles to maintain order, and it was only the tact of the
S.B.O. that saved the lives of several of the wilder spirits.

CHAPTER IX

AFTER THE news of Otto's death Loveday seemed to
retire into a world of his own. He rarely spoke to the
others, and when he did it was to utter some vague defiant
threat against *them.* Who *they* were, the others could never
really understand. It was not merely the Germans, it was
some malignant force that worked secretly in the darkness
to undermine his significance.

Peter and John were less affected than the others by his
gloom. They worked in the tunnel during the day and spent
the long light evenings in the theatre. Hugo and Saunders,
who saw more of him, were depressed by his long silences
more than they had been by his earlier noisy argument.
It seemed as though, even when silent, he could cast
his spell over them, and they lived in a state of nervous
anticipation.

Then, for no apparent reason, he announced that in future
he would prepare his own food.

"But you can't do that," Peter said. "It's not economical."

"It's better than the other thing."

"What other thing?"

"You know perfectly well what I mean."

"But I don't know, Loveday."

"Then you take me for a bigger fool than I thought you
did."

Saunders as usual tried to joke him out of his mood but
he was obdurate. He insisted that one food parcel out of
five should be given to him to do with as he pleased. He
cooked privately, in private tins, and ate at unusual times.
His horror of eating anything that had been prepared by

232

the others made it obvious that he suspected them of poisoning him.

Shortly after this, as Peter was returning from the tunnel, Hugo met him and suggested a walk round the circuit. Peter could tell by his manner that this was more than an ordinary request for company.

"How are you getting on with the tunnel?" Hugo asked.

"We shan't be out before the end of the month. It's pretty slow."

"I can't understand why you do it." Hugo smoothed his hair. "There's very little chance of getting away with it —now, honestly, is there?"

"We shouldn't be trying if there weren't a chance."

"Come on," Hugo said. "Be honest. How much chance d'you think you've got?"

"Ninety per cent."

"Of getting out of the camp, yes. But what's the use of that? Look at the last lot—all brought back except two. And they were killed. That's a fine result, if you like."

"I still think it's worth it," Peter said.

"Why?"

Peter walked in silence for a moment, wondering what to say; wondering how to describe his longing to get back to flying and the fear of flying, how to describe the challenge of that tall wire fence. It was too much like shooting a line. It seemed pointless to talk of freedom, of life in the world beyond the wire—Hugo probably wanted that as much as he did. But Hugo was prepared to wait for it. He gave it up. "It's a way of passing the time," he said.

"A pretty futile way of passing the time, I should say."

"But what are you doing?" Peter asked. "You always seem to be doing something, but to boil it down, what do you actually do?"

"Oh, I'm learning quite a lot."

"What?"

Hugo laughed. "How to pass the time, for one thing. I seem to have spent most of my life doing that. Y'know, my aunt leaves me over a hundred thousand when she dies. All I have to do is wait for it. Now I should look pretty silly if I crawled out of a tunnel and got a bullet in my guts, shouldn't I?"

"I suppose so. That's the aunt with the cat, isn't it?"

"Yes, she's the only relative I've got. I hate the old bitch. She's inherited all the family property bit by bit and now she owns everything—because of a damn' silly will my grandfather made."

"How old is she?"

"About eighty. It can't be long now. I just make the time pass as quickly as I can. That's all most of you tunnellers are doing—you say so yourself. Some of you get so fond of your damn' tunnels that you forget what they're for, and just go on digging for the fun of it. I reckon some of you dread the day when you have to come to the end of them."

It's no use trying to tell him, Peter thought. I suppose he's right in a way. I do spend more time than I need in the tunnel. He wondered why Hugo had suggested the walk. Surely not to talk about tunnels—Hugo, who could not possibly be less interested. Or was it all an elaborate bluff? Was he going to ask for a place in it now that they were nearly finished?

"I'm rather worried about Loveday," Hugo said. "That's why I wanted to talk to you, Pete. I found a knife in his bed the other day."

"Well, there's nothing in that. You should see the stuff I find in my bed sometimes."

"No—I'm serious. He hadn't just left it there by accident. I saw him hiding it." There was something in Hugo's voice that made Peter realise that he meant what he said. Hugo, usually so detached, was not one to panic easily over a thing like this. "I taxed him with it," he continued.

"He told me some garbled yarn about having to protect himself."

"Protect himself? From whom?"

"I don't know. You know how he is. He got all mysterious and then shut up like a clam. He makes me nervous."

"What d'you think we ought to do?"

"I think we should see Stewart about it. Loveday should be where he can be properly looked after."

"I saw the S.B.O. the morning after he had that fit," Peter said. "It's no good. The goons say he's not ill enough to go to hospital. They suspect he's swinging the lead for a 'repat.'"

"Then I think he should be moved to another mess."

"It seems a little like admitting defeat."

"Either he or John should move." Hugo seemed emphatic about this.

"Why John in particular?"

"He seems to upset him more than the others. It seems that he somehow can't bear to see John reading. It drives him into a frenzy."

"He seems to be getting worse since Otto went," Peter admitted.

"I'm sure of it."

"What d'you suggest?"

"Either he or John should go. I think there'll be trouble if they're not separated."

Peter did not reply. He was still trying to remember Loveday's particular animosity towards John. He certainly hadn't noticed it; Loveday seemed to treat them all with equal distrust.

"What about it?" Hugo said. "I'm worried about him, Pete."

"It won't be for much longer," Peter said. "We'll be gone by the end of the month."

"You can't bank on that."

"All right—I'll go and see Stewart," Peter said. "We've had him for nearly four months. It's time somebody else had a go."

When they got back to the barrack block they found the place in an uproar. There was a strong smell of burning wood and the room was filled with smoke. The prisoners were crowding towards the end of the block, towards their mess.

They pushed their way through and found Saunders, his normally red face a dirty grey, standing over a pile of burned bedding which lay in the middle of the floor.

"What the hell's wrong?" Peter asked.

"That fool Loveday! He set fire to the bedding and then threw all John's books on to it. Flames were damn' nearly up to the ceiling. Dancing round it, he was, and singing at the top of his voice."

"Where is he now?"

"They took him to the hospital."

"Where's John?"

"Dunno—haven't seen him since lunch."

Peter knew a moment's panic, then remembered that John had gone straight down to the theatre. "We'd better clear the place up," he said.

"Mad as a hatter," Saunders said. "Singing and dancing round and flinging the books on. He nearly killed me—got me by the throat. The place was so thick with smoke anyway, the other chaps hadn't noticed anything. I walked in and there he was."

"Never mind," Peter said. "Perhaps we'll get a little peace for a change."

For Peter the next few weeks sped by remarkably quickly. They had been prisoners for nearly four months, and had by now acquired some of the equanimity that he had so admired in the older kriegies. The moods of depression and desperation still visited them, but they had learned to control this feeling, to consider its effect on their fellow prisoners. Their tunnel, now the only escape route undiscovered by the Germans, was moving steadily nearer and nearer to the wire, and the evenings, without Loveday, had become periods of quiet enjoyment.

Oddly enough, the nearer he got to escape, the more virtue Peter found in the prison life. He found companionship, unselfishness and a certain personal freedom such as he had never known before. But, he told himself, he was only a recent prisoner. The novelty of this would wear off, the lack of responsibility would take its toll. He must push on with his plans for the journey, work to ensure that his escape from the camp was a permanent one; and yet at the same time make the most of imprisonment's rather negative virtues. He was busy on the designs for the scenery of *A Midsummer Night's Dream* and John was learning the part of Lysander. Saunders had been roped in to play Bottom while even Hugo had roused himself sufficiently to accept the role of Peter Quince The Carpenter.

"Come on, Saunders," Hugo said. "*Let us hear, sweet Bottom.*"

"I'd like to do Act One again," Saunders said. "The beginning of Scene Two."

"O.K. Will you prompt, Pete?" Hugo handed him the book and cleared his throat. "*Is all our company here?*"

"*You were best to call them generally, man by man, according to the scrip.*" Saunders spoke in a false, hollow voice, absolutely without inflection.

"*Appel* up," John said. He was copying a map of Yugoslavia that they had borrowed from the Escape Committee.

Hugo ignored him. "*Here is the scroll of every man's name, which is thought fit, through all Athens, to play in our interlude before the Duke and Duchess on their wedding night.*"

"It's not *on their wedding night*," Peter said. "It's *on his wedding day at night.*"

"Must be a misprint," Saunders said.

"That's what it says here."

"It doesn't scan properly," Hugo said. "Why *on his wedding day at night*? After all, they're both getting married. I'll say *on their wedding night*."

Saunders was horrified. "You can't do that—you've got to say it according to the script."

"Why?"

"Well, it's Shakespeare!"

"Let's rewrite the whole thing," John said. "Do it kriegie fashion, like this:

> "Say, bum, is everyone on *appel*?
> Better call the roll, *Was haben Sie*?
> These are the bods, they all act well,
> *Blond genug*—what part's for me?"

"It's no use," Saunders said. "I can't work in this madhouse. We'll do it on the circuit in the morning."

"You've got weeks to learn it in," Hugo said, "and nothing else to do. You'll get stale if you learn it too soon."

"That's true." Saunders said it with relief. "I think I'll get on with making that oven." He got out his sheets of tin and started hammering.

"It's been pretty quiet since Loveday left," Peter said.

"What did you say?" John shouted.

"I SAID IT'S BEEN PRETTY QUIET SINCE LOVEDAY LEFT!"

"I wonder how he's getting on!"

"He's still in the hospital," Hugo told him. "I called in there this morning. The M.O.'s trying to get him sent to Obermassfeld but the goons won't move. He's told them he won't be responsible if they keep him here."

"I miss him, you know, in a way." Saunders stopped hammering and sat astride the bench. "He's a good chap in a way, you know."

"He's too selfish for prison life," John said.

"Oh, I don't know."

"He isn't selfish enough, that's the trouble." Peter fetched his drawing materials from the shelf above his head. "He's too interested in other people's affairs. It's a sort of generosity—he wants to share his thoughts all the time."

"It's selfishness really," John said. "He can't bear not to be in on everything."

"It's uncertainty," Hugo said. "He wants to be reassured all the time. He wants to feel that people need him."

"He didn't go the right way about it then."

"He's a nice chap, really," Saunders insisted. "He only burned your books because he thought you'd be better off without 'em."

"Thanks—that's a comfort."

"I suppose we could have done more to help him," Peter said.

"It wouldn't have been any use," Hugo told him. "It's in the man—it's nothing to do with us."

"I wonder who'll take his place." Saunders pushed his woollen cap to the back of his head. "They won't leave us with only four in the mess."

"There'll be a new purge in soon," Hugo said. "We'll be eight then."

"More's the pity." Peter was working on a design for Snout's costume; a Red Cross packing-case suspended from the shoulders round the waist, and painted to represent the Wall. "I reckon four is just about the right number for a mess."

"We shall get four more when the next purge comes in." Hugo was emphatic about this. "Now that Loveday's gone there's no excuse for only having six in the mess."

"You'll need *six* more," John said. "And a new Lysander."

"Go on, you haven't a hope," Saunders said.

"That's what you think."

"How far've you got since you opened it up again?"

"Thirty feet."

"When d'you think you'll break?"

"Another week should see us through," John said.

"Go on!"

"It's a fact," Peter told him.

"How are you going?" Saunders seemed, only now, to think it possible that they were really going.

"I'm going as an Italian," Peter said. "John's going as my daughter."

"Stow it!"

"Honestly. We've thought the whole thing out. We'll walk at night, and if anyone sees us we just go into a clinch in a hedge or up against a wall—and no one would dream of disturbing us. The most natural thing in the world."

"*Un*matural," Hugo said. "It's incest."

"I think they've got something," Saunders said. "What about clothes?"

"I'm making a skirt out of a greatcoat," John said. "I'll wear a sort of sweater with a built-up brassière, and a scarf round my head."

"That's why you're letting your hair grow . . ." Saunders stopped in admiration. "You're pretty wide, you two. Where are you making for?"

"Yugoslavia."

"You might get away with it," Saunders said. "You're both dark enough to pass as Italians. It's the sort of stupid effort that would succeed."

"I shouldn't be——"

The whole room was silenced by the rifle shot. From outside, close at hand. The silence was shattered again by two more shots, one after the other; and then the shrill eerie whistle of the guard and the chatter of a machine-gun.

"Someone's climbing the wire," John said.

Peter shivered. The silent room was drowned in a flood of conversation. "Shut up!" someone shouted; and they all listened for further shots.

"It came from behind the *abort*," Saunders whispered.

"No—I think it was from the other side."

"It was this side, I think—pretty loud."

"I thought it came from near the hospital," Hugo said.

They listened again, but heard only the rain beating on the shutters and the moaning of the wind round the roof of the barrack block.

"Rotten night to try the wire." Saunders laughed nervously.

"It's the only sort of night," John said. "I suppose this means another delay."

"Depends what it was," Peter said. "May have been some trigger-happy goon shooting at his own shadow. Let's hope so, anyway."

Peter was dreaming. He lay on his back on the tough uncut grass of the Downs and far far below he could hear the sea rubbing itself against the white chalk base of the cliffs. At his side the girl (It was never Pat. Why did he never dream of Pat?), cool in a summer frock, leaned on bare brown arms and faced the sun. Under her frock her legs were long and smooth and brown. He could not see them but he knew it. The sun was on her face, reflecting from the slight moistness of her brow and nose and upper lip, making a halo of her hair. Behind her head was the far unfathomable blue of the sky with small white clouds like thistledown sailing slowly and steadily in from the sea.

When she turned to look at him her eyes were as blue and as deep as the sea and as she stooped towards him he saw the slow sweet curve of her breasts.

Suddenly she was without her frock, smooth and cool and

Q

warm at the same time. She bent to kiss him. The sound
of the sea grew louder and everything was warm and damp
and cold and damp, and when he awoke it was slowly and
warmly and happily as though it had really happened. He
lay in the narrow bunk in the darkness, trying to recapture
the vision until, suddenly, at the far end of the long room
he heard someone crying in his sleep, "Christ, we're on
fire! Jesus, Jesus! Jesus! . . . Bale out! Bale out! . . .
Jesus Christ! Jesus Christ, Jesus Christ! . . ."

CHAPTER X

THE NEXT morning, as they were having breakfast, Stewart came into the mess.

"'Morning, chaps."

"'Morning, Stewart," Peter said. "What was going on last night? Had any news?"

"Yes." Stewart was unusually solemn. "I have, as a matter of fact. They shot Loveday last night."

There was a shocked silence.

"Who did?" Saunders said. "The goons?"

"The S.B.O. just told me about it," Stewart said. "Apparently one of our orderlies had been told to stay with him the whole time, but he went off to his room to get some cigarettes and while he was away Loveday climbed up on to the roof in his pyjamas."

"Blimey, it was raining," Saunders said.

"He got down off the roof," Stewart continued, "and then tried to climb the wire by the gate. A sentry saw him and told him to get down. Loveday ignored him so the sentry shot him through the stomach."

"Was he trying to escape?" Saunders asked.

"I don't think so. The S.B.O. said that he was singing and shouting at the top of his voice."

"The bloody murderer," Saunders said.

"One of you must attend the funeral," Stewart told them. "It's to-morrow afternoon. Whichever of you it is must wear service dress and a cap. The Germans are giving him military honours."

When Stewart had gone the four men sat back and looked at one another.

"I'm not going," Saunders said. "Oh, no. I don't like funerals. Anyway . . ." he hesitated. "I'd rather not go, that's all."

"I'll go," Hugo said. "Be rather nice to get away from barbed wire for a few hours."

Peter cleared his throat. "I don't like to claim any privilege or anything like that—but it would be jolly useful if John or I went. We could have a scout round outside and get the lie of the land."

"It's obvious," Saunders said. "One of you two must go."

"Sorry," Hugo said. "I hadn't thought of that. You'd better toss up between you."

"You'd better go, Pete. You're in the R.A.F. Besides, there isn't a decent army uniform in the place."

"I'll have to borrow the kit from somewhere," Peter said. "I wonder if Stewart would lend me his tunic."

"Wing commander for a day," Saunders said.

As Peter went down to the tunnel that morning he felt as though someone had given him a present. To go beyond the wire even for a few hours, to go through the village again and see people living normal lives. He tried to stifle this joy, to realise that he was going to Loveday's funeral, then to excuse it by reminding himself that he was going to get the lie of the land for the tunnel break; but it was no good. He felt more as though he had won a sweepstake.

The tunnel was nearly finished, and as he lay hacking away at the hard, tenacious clay he felt that nothing could now stop them from getting out.

They had recently come to a layer of large, flat, smooth stones which, Tyson said, had probably once formed the bed of a river. The ground was even wetter here, but once beyond it they had begun to drive the tunnel upwards towards the surface where it was drier. But the air was bad at the head of the tunnel owing to the upward slope, and Peter was forced to crawl back to the bottom of the slope at intervals for air. He had just returned to the face for another spell of work when the lamp at his head guttered out and filled the tunnel with its acrid smoke.

I'll crawl back and have a chat with John, he thought. Give the air time to clear a bit.

He crawled back to the lower shaft where John should have been working, but there was no one there. Thinking this odd, he climbed the ladder in the darkness and edged along the upper tunnel. There was no light, only the darkness and the silence, and he had a sudden fear and quickened his crawl towards the chamber at the base of the upper shaft, fighting hard to keep from utter panic. He thought that he was alone, that the others had gone and sealed him down. He could hear himself panting in the darkness as he pulled his body through the puddled clay.

Suddenly he bumped into John. "What the hell's wrong?" he asked. "Why are all the lights out?"

"The goons are searching the cookhouse," John whispered. "I was coming to fetch you. The chaps have shut the trap down—we'll have to stay here until the search is over."

"Hope they don't call an *appel*." Tyson's voice came softly out of the darkness. "We've had it if they do."

"D'you think they suspect anything?"

"I doubt it," Tyson whispered. "Just a routine check, I should think. It's getting bloody cold down here."

Peter realised that he, too, was cold; that the damp clay was drawing all the warmth from his body. He shivered. "I'll go for a crawl up the tunnel, I think."

"I'll go with you," John said.

They stopped at the top of the lower shaft for breath. "How long shall we have to stay down here, I wonder?" Peter said.

"It'll be lunchtime soon—they're bound to pack it in by then."

They sat opposite one another in the upper tunnel, their legs dangling down the shaft.

"Getting pretty stuffy down here, isn't it?" Peter said.

"I could do with a smoke."

"That'd make it worse. God knows what it'll be like when there are about forty of us lying down here waiting to get out."

"We'll have the exit open then, that will let some air in," John said. "I'm glad we shall be up at the front end, in more ways than one."

"So am I," Peter said. "I don't think this air will last much longer."

"It'll see us out," John said. "There's enough down here to last for hours."

"Let's go back and see what's happening." Peter wanted to get back near the shaft, away from the compressing darkness of the tunnel. They felt their way back to where Tyson crouched at the bottom of the upper shaft.

"There was a hell of a row going on just now," he told them. "It sounded as though the whole German army were in the cookhouse."

"Probably a blitz search," John said.

"The air's pretty bad down here." Tyson sounded worried. "We'd better give 'em a bit longer, then if we hear nothing we'll assume that the goons have cleared everyone out. If we lift the trap carefully we can have a look round and get some air."

For the next half-hour they lay panting in the darkness of the tunnel. The air was getting worse, so bad that it was advisable not to move about. By huddling together in the chamber at the bottom of the shaft they were able to generate some warmth. Tyson had disconnected the tube from the air pump and worked the pump to change the air at intervals.

Peter sat with his back propped against the wall of the chamber and hoped that the Germans would not find them. He realised now that he had banked everything on this tunnel; that the nearer they got to breaking out the more important the tunnel had become. It was strange this, because ever since Loveday had gone he had almost enjoyed his imprisonment.

And now Loveday was dead. He wondered what had been in Loveday's mind to make him climb the wire like that. They had been talking about him when it happened, or about that time. He thought of their remarks when they had heard the shots, of how they had wondered if it would affect their tunnel—this tunnel. And now he was dead. Perhaps it was better that way. He comforted himself with the old cliché—as though death could be better than any sort of life. What had possessed the man to climb out of the hospital window on to the roof, in his pyjamas? Singing and shouting, Stewart had said. Then he had climbed down to the ground, and crossed to the wire. Still singing, he had started to climb the fence. The outside sentry, walking down the wire, had stopped opposite him, and told him to get down. The sentry had warned him that he would shoot, but Loveday took no notice. It had been raining, and Peter could picture the wild figure, pyjamas too short in the leg, hair plastered over his face, climbing the wire and singing. Singing while the rain soaked into his thin pyjamas. What had he been singing? A hymn perhaps. The sentry, in his panic, had shot him through the stomach. Three shots, and then the machine-gun from the tower had started up—firing blindly, hysterically, into the darkness. And Loveday, his entrails pushed through his back, had stopped his singing.

Peter felt sick inside. Perhaps it had been partly his fault. Perhaps if they had been more understanding. . . . He pushed the thought away; but it was no good. He must accept some of the blame. He could have tried a little harder. He remembered Hugo's words: "It was in the man—it was nothing to do with us." But he could not accept them. How bound up they were, how dependent. How impossible to live a life "free from all businesses."

What was it Marcus Aurelius had said? *At what time soever thou wilt, it is in thy power to retire into thyself, and to be at rest, and free from all businesses?*

"Half an hour must be up," John said.

"I was thinking the same thing," Tyson said. "I'll go and have a shufti." He climbed the ladder, but came down a few minutes later. "I'd forgotten—you can't open the trap from the inside. The boiler has to be moved."

"Then we'll have to wait," John said.

Peter thought of the argument they had had about the sentry; of how Saunders had blamed him, saying it was murder, and of how he, Peter, had made excuses for the man. Was the German to be blamed? How could he have known that Loveday was round the bend? Supposing he had been sane—supposing the sentry had let him climb down the outside of the wire, and had led him back inside again? Someone else would have tried it sooner or later. Eventually someone fully clothed under his pyjamas would have tried to climb the wire. A handful of armed men controlling a thousand prisoners must shoot when they say they'll shoot, otherwise they would have no control. He could have shot to maim, Saunders had said—in the arm, or the leg. Hardly, on a wet and stormy night like that. Besides, the man was frightened. Who would not be frightened of a wild and singing figure, climbing the wire in the rain. Poor old Loveday, what a way to end your life.

"It must be well after lunchtime," John said.

"I expect the goons have called another *appel*," Tyson said.

"What'll happen when they find we're missing?"

"They won't, if the chaps can manage it. They should be able to cover our absence all right—after all, we're only three."

That's what it is, Peter thought, they must be on *appel*. The others will cover us all right. They *must* cover us, we can't be discovered now. A few more days and we shall be away. They can't possibly discover us now.

He thought of Loveday again, wished that he could honestly acquit himself of all responsibility. But he could not. He could not retire into himself. Loveday, the Russian prisoners, Otto's torture and death—these things were everyone's responsibility. But what to do about it? The thing was too big to start at the top. If everyone started at the bottom now, if everyone made certain that his own personal relationships were not tainted with the cruelty . . . If only Loveday were alive that he could start at once— start a small pocket of resistance against the cruelty that enslaved the world. He imagined millions of small pockets of resistance working upwards from the bottom, millions of men working outwards from within the cruelty, refusing to retire into themselves.

They heard the thud of footsteps on the floor above, the scrape of the stove being moved. The trap was lifted. The head and shoulders of one of the stooges appeared in the opening.

"Sorry, you chaps. It was the Swedish Commission. Some Red Cross blokes came in to inspect the cookhouse. We though we'd never get rid of them. You'd better hurry up —the goons have laid on a special lunch."

"We've saved your lunch." Hugo indicated the two bowls of barley soup, two small pieces of raw-looking sausage and two rolls of white bread which stood on the table.

"The tea's still hot," Saunders said. "I put the jug on the stove."

"I suppose you've heard the news," Hugo said.

"About the Swedish Commission?" Peter asked.

"About the move."

"Move?" Peter stopped eating. The sausage felt like lead in his throat. He knew before he said it what Hugo was about to say.

"We're going in about four purges. *Stalag-Luft III*, I think they call it. Supposed to be a pretty good camp."

"When are we going?" Peter managed to ask. Perhaps there would be time to finish the tunnel before the move. Perhaps there was still a chance.

"First thing Monday morning. We're going in four purges," Hugo repeated. "Personally I shall be jolly glad to get out of the place."

Peter could have murdered him. He sat in front of the special lunch, feeling that everything was finished. To have been discovered would have been bad enough; but to be moved to another camp just before breaking was the last straw. He turned to John.

"We'll just have to leave it, that's all," John said. "There's another week's work at least. We can't possibly do it before the move." He spoke lightly, as though the tunnel were of no importance; but Peter knew what it meant to him, knew the control he must be exercising to be able to speak like this.

"It's jolly tough luck," Saunders said. "Especially after you'd got as far as that."

"Is the whole camp going?" Peter could hardly believe it, even now.

"Every man jack," Hugo said.

"Who's coming into this camp after us?" Peter asked.

"They say it's not going to be used as a military camp any more," Hugo said. "Too insanitary. They'll probably turn it over to the *Gestapo*."

"What a find, for anyone who does come in!" Saunders chuckled. "A ready-made tunnel, just waiting for 'em."

"Don't talk about it," John said. He opened a book and began to read.

"Why did it happen so suddenly?" Peter wanted to get it straight.

"Orders from Berlin," Hugo said. "After the last escape, I expect."

"But that was weeks ago."

"The news just got through, I expect. Everyone has to be evacuated within forty-eight hours."

"I bet it was the Swedish Commission," Saunders said. "I bet they said the place wasn't fit to live in."

"No, it wouldn't be that," Hugo said. "They wouldn't work so fast on that recommendation. The Berlin rumour seems more like it."

"It's definite we're going?" Peter still thought there might be a hope.

"The day after to-morrow," Hugo said.

Having been prepared for disappointment for so long, Peter was able to hide it. "You can go to the funeral if you like," he told Hugo. "There's no point in my going now."

"No, it's O.K.," Hugo said. "You've got the uniform together now. You'd better go."

"What's *Stalag-Luft III* like?" Peter asked. "Is it a new camp?"

"I think so—it's in a pine forest, I believe."

Peter could imagine it. Virgin ground. They'd get in early and stake their claim for a tunnel. Get cracking as soon as they arrived. The last tunnel had been good experience, now they would make one on their own. Keep it small and take no unnecessary risks. "Which purge are we going in?"

"The first. We leave at eight o'clock in the morning— we'd better start getting packed right away."

"I hope there's a theatre," Saunders said. "Don't want to waste all that energy I used learning my part."

Stewart came in with a handful of letters. "Last post you'll get for a few weeks—better make the most of it."

"Is it a fact we're all going?" Peter asked.

"Yes," Stewart said. "Rotten luck on you chaps. You'd nearly finished, hadn't you?"

"We were going out next Friday," Peter said. "What's the new camp like?"

"Wooden huts," Stewart said. "Eight in a room. By the way—the funeral party meets at two o'clock at the main gate." He put the letters down on the table. Among the official letter-forms was one envelope deeply edged with black. It was addressed to Hugo. Stewart looked at the letter, then at Hugo, but said nothing.

· They watched Hugo as he opened it, watched his face drain of colour as he read.

"Who is it?" Saunders said. "Your aunt?"

Hugo fought hard to control himself. "No," he said, in a strangled voice. "It's the cat."

"What a day!" Saunders said. "What a bloody day!"

As he sat polishing his buttons for the funeral Peter had an idea. The Russian compound. Why couldn't a group of them drive a shaft up from the middle of the tunnel and come out in the Russian compound? They could hide there until the others had gone and then complete the tunnel at their leisure. He pulled on his clogs and hurried down to Tyson's room.

Tyson was sitting alone at the table, sewing bars of chocolate into a watertight packet made from a rubber groundsheet.

"I've got an idea," Peter said.

"It's all right," Tyson said. "There are stooges out."

"Why not come up in the Russian compound?" Peter said. "Hide there until the others have gone?"

"We'd thought of that." Tyson's smile was almost gentle. "I've just spoken to their head man about it, but he won't play. Says they'd all be shot if we were caught. I expect they would be too. He even went so far as to say he'd tell the goons if we tried it."

"Need the Russians know?"

"They know where the tunnel is, they've heard us digging. They'll be on the look-out for it now. Can't blame them in a way, you know."

"I don't blame them," Peter said. "It's just rotten luck."

"I'm going to hide down there," Tyson said, without looking up from his sewing.

Peter waited.

"I'll stay down there till you've all gone, then I'll come up from our end. There's just a chance the compound will be left unguarded."

"You can't get out from inside," Peter said. "We found that out this morning."

"I've arranged for the Pole who drives the night-cart to come in and let me out."

Peter felt a deepening of his admiration for the man. He certainly hadn't wasted time in useless regret since he had learned of the move. And here he was calmly sewing food into waterproof bags, giving his life into the hands of a man he hardly knew.

"Supposing he doesn't come?" Peter said.

Tyson went on sewing.

"He might be too scared," Peter said. "Or there might be Germans here."

"It's worth the risk," Tyson said.

"Is there room for two?" Peter, as he said it, felt that he was abandoning John; but there obviously wouldn't be room for three.

"I thought you'd ask that," Tyson said, "and the answer is no. There's not enough air for two. I've talked it over with the Committee and they've decided it's a scheme for one."

Peter met the rest of the funeral party—there was one representative from each block—at the main gate and, after the usual German delay, they set off by car to the cemetery.

He sat next to Mueller in the back of the small German car and thought miserably of the fruitless months he had spent slowly driving himself forward through the heavy clay. Hugo was right, it was just so much wasted effort.

They did not talk on the way to the cemetery. Peter felt that Mueller was anxious not to discuss the shooting, and for his own part he preferred the silence. As they drove through the poor-looking streets of the Polish town he thought how different it would have been had they not been moving to another camp. What he now saw with little more than ordinary interest he would then have seen with an eye to cover, an eye to the safest way of passing through the town. He was on parole now, outside the wire, bound by honour not to escape. That's how it was with all privileges; the theatre, the church, funerals—all received on conditions, all accepted with a slight feeling of guilt.

They met the cortège party just inside the gates of the churchyard. There was a detachment of armed German soldiers drawn up on one side of the gravel path. An R.A.F. service cap surrounded by a wreath of leaves rested on the top of the plain wooden coffin in the horse-drawn cart.

Peter and the other prisoners lifted down the coffin, and followed the British padre. The soldiers formed up behind them.

By the side of the open grave the padre, his white surplice tugging in the breeze, read the service, while the German escort, uncomprehending, stood at ease in two ranks. Peter wondered whether the guard who had done the shooting was there. Probably not—probably sent on leave as a reward for his efficiency.

The padre was reading from his small black book. "*I held my tongue, and spake nothing: I kept silence, yes, even from good words; but it was pain and grief to me;*

"*My heart was hot within me, and while I was thus musing the fire kindled: and at the last I spake with my tongue;*

"*Lord, let me know mine end, and the number of my days: that I may be certified how long I have to live . . .*"

Peter stood and looked at the coffin lying across the ropes

by the side of the open grave. They had not been able to cover it with a flag. The cap with its faded gold and red badge looked strange surrounded by the German wreath. He wondered to whom the cap belonged.

He came to himself again. They were lowering the coffin into the grave and the padre was sprinkling the dark earth on to the hollow wood. Peter took a handful of earth and threw it on. "*Earth to earth, ashes to ashes, dust to dust . . .*" the padre read from the book. As Peter rubbed his hand on his trouser-leg he tried to think of Loveday, to remember the kindliness behind the restless fear. But the dark gaping hole reminded him too much of the tunnel. Of Tyson shut down there; struggling for breath, wondering if the Pole would keep his word. He was safe enough, Peter supposed. No man would be evil enough to leave a man to die. But what a risk to take. He was secretly glad that Tyson had refused to take him. Glad.

There would be another tunnel. He must learn to treat each failure as a preparation, a preparation for the next attempt. There was no giving up now. He would go on digging until he had dug his way out.

The padre finished reading. The wailing notes of a German trumpet haunted the sad air of the Polish church-yard. The rifles crashed. One by one the British officers stepped forward and saluted the grave. Slowly the funeral party walked past tortured iron and carved stone towards the cars which waited to take them back to the camp; back to release from parole, perhaps to another tunnel from another, unknown camp.

THE END